REAL·HE~~~~~~~~~~~~~~~

of the North West

Pub Interiors of Special Historic Interest

Edited by **Geoff Brandwood**

With photography by **Michael Slaughter**

CAMPAIGN FOR REAL ALE

Based on CAMRA's Inventories of Historic Pub Interiors for North West England and the Isle of Man

Produced by CAMRA's Pub Heritage Group
www.heritagepubs.org.uk
E info.pubheritage@camra.org.uk

For CAMRA Books
Head of Publishing: Simon Hall
Project Manager: Julie Hudson
Sales and Marketing: Chris Lewis

Book design/typography: Dale Tomlinson
Maps: Alan and Julie Snook
Plan (p. 13): Stephen Bere

Published by the Campaign for Real Ale Ltd.
230 Hatfield Road, St Albans
Hertfordshire AL1 4LW
www.camra.org.uk/books

© Campaign for Real Ale Ltd. 2017

First published 2017

ISBN 978-1-85249-345-5

A CIP catalogue record for this book is available from
the British Library

Printed and bound in the United Kingdom by
Cambrian Printers Ltd, Aberystwyth

Photo credits
All photographs are by Michael Slaughter
LRPS unless otherwise indicated.

AD Andrew Davison
GB Geoff Brandwood
MC Michael Croxford
NL Neil Lloyd
PK Peter Kelly

Cover and title-page photos
Front: The magnificent lobby area at
the Philharmonic Dining Rooms,
Liverpool, *c*.1900 (GB)
Rear: The rear snug area at the
Black Horse, Preston, 1929 (GB)
Title page: Modes of transport from different
ages in early 20th-century painted glass at
Peter Kavanagh's, Liverpool

Contents

Introduction

Pubs to Cherish

Real Heritage Pubs of the North West celebrates pub interiors in north-west England (plus the Isle of Man) which CAMRA has identified as having special historic interest. They represent an important aspect of the area's cultural and built heritage and quite a number are true national treasures.

That said, they account for only 2% or so of all the pubs in the area – why is that so? A major reason, of course, is that pub interiors have always been subject to change. The only pubs which are exactly the same as the day they opened are ones which came into being in the last few years. The pace of change, though, accelerated dramatically from the 1960s. Then there began a mania for opening out, faddish theming, image change and general trashing. Consequently, many a pub suffered makeovers during which most, if not all, vestiges of original or early features were lost.

The irony here is that interest in historic buildings has never been greater. Lots of us are fascinated by our built heritage and spend time visiting historic buildings of many kinds. But it is only in recent years, and largely as a result of CAMRA's efforts, that pub interiors have come to be valued by mainstream conservationists. It was CAMRA that picked up the baton on behalf of our pub heritage, filling the gaps in knowledge of what is out there and actively seeking to protect what is left. It has worked closely with Historic England (formerly English Heritage) to gain statutory protection for the most important examples on our inventories through the statutory listing process. Nonetheless there are still losses either through closure or change by insensitive owners eager to tear them apart.

This is the eighth in a series of regional guides to our best heritage pubs and draws on many years of work by CAMRA members to track down and record those which have escaped the attention of the modernisers and 'improvers'. We hope it will help to increase the awareness about their importance. Enjoy!

The Marble Arch Inn, in central Manchester, was built in 1888 and its interior has a spectacular display of ceramic work. The counter was evidently longer originally

What Shaped Pubs in the North West

In the beginning

Most early public houses were literally just that – ordinary houses whose owners opened up a room or two to sell drink to neighbours. All that was needed was somewhere to store the merchandise, someone to serve it and somewhere for customers to drink it. Pub keeping was a family business and, especially in the countryside, usually part-time and combined with, say, farming, carting, blacksmithing or some other trade. Nearly all these very homely pubs have gone now but we can still see a few vestiges in the pubs within this guide.

The very simply appointed Limeburners Arms, Nether Kellet, Lancashire (p. 48) is still linked to a working farm: it only opens in the evenings as the licensee runs the latter during the daytime, a pattern that may well reflect what happened in many rural establishments. At Gawsworth, Cheshire, the Harrington Arms (p. 20) had a farm attached until recently but the two are now separate businesses. The Scotch Piper, Lydiate (p. 114), is widely considered Lancashire's oldest pub, and within its timber-framed walls you can still get some sense of the rustic simplicity in days gone by. If you visit the venerable Black Lion, Barthomley, Cheshire (p. 18), wish away everything apart from the right-hand room to envisage how it would have been in former days.

The simply appointed public bar at the Scotch Piper, Lydiate, reputedly historic Lancashire's oldest pub (GB)

Inns and taverns

The other kinds of establishment up until the early 19th century were the tavern and the inn. The former existed only in larger towns, catering for the more prosperous customer by serving wine and food. They were never common and no former taverns appear to survive in the North West although Mr Thomas's Chop House in Manchester (p. 65) perhaps retains something of the atmosphere of such establishments. Inns provided meals and accommodation for better-off travellers along with stabling for their horses. Inevitably they have been greatly modified but places whose origins go back centuries include the Falcon, Chester (not in this guide), and the Olde Man and Scythe, Bolton. The Dockray Hall, Penrith, Cumbria, is known to have become an inn in 1719 (haylofts for the stabling can still be seen on the west wing).

The Dockray Hall, Penrith, Cumbria, became an inn in 1719. Note the carriage entrance on the right (GB)

The golden age

The pub as we know today is mostly a Victorian creation. The first part of the 19th century saw the widespread adoption of counter service and the hand-pumped beer engine, heralding the change from an essentially domestic environment into a form of shop which could handle a greater volume of trade. Just as most rural pubs once catered primarily for the agricultural labourer, vast numbers of urban pubs were fairly basic establishments for the working man. In industrial areas especially, pubs afforded welcome refreshment after a shift down the pit, in the steelworks, or a day of other heavy labour. Such pubs were a good deal more numerous than they are today with so many towns and cities justifying, almost literally, the epithet about

7

Inside Britain's most magnificent pub, the Philharmonic Dining Rooms, Liverpool, dating from the golden age of pub-building about 1900 (GB)

The Stork Hotel, Birkenhead, has a spectacular glazed front of, perhaps, 1905 (GB)

Mosaic at the entrance to a Wigan pub catering for railway travellers

pubs, 'one on every street corner'. The tiny Circus Tavern in central Manchester (p. 63) is a remarkable survivor as a tiny urban pub. All this was overlain with the complexities of Victorian societal structures so that multiple rooms or screened off compartments were the norm to accommodate the social and economic distinctions between customers, even within the working population.

From the early Victorian period, under the influence of social reformers and the powerful Temperance lobby (see pp. 88–9), a drive to improve public houses gained ground. This enhanced the multi-room principle with its ability to offer a choice of 'better' rooms and thus attract a respectable clientele who would pay slightly more than public bar drinkers. The years around 1900 proved to be a high point of pub building both in terms of numbers and sheer quality. Nowhere is this better illustrated than in Liverpool whose immense prosperity as a global trading city led to the building of two of the most superlative pubs in the land – the Philharmonic Dining Rooms (p. 104) and the Vines (p. 107). Other very fine Liverpool pubs from the late Victorian/Edwardian years, enriched with elaborate glasswork, carved woodwork and ceramics, are the Central, Crown Hotel, Midland Hotel and Lion Tavern. Other shining examples from the time are to be found in Birkenhead (Stork Hotel), Eccles (Lamb Hotel and the Grapes), Manchester (Marble Arch), Preston (Black Horse), and Wigan (Springfield). The now rather anachronistic word 'hotel' still attached to some of these names shows how pubs commonly provided accommodation. Another example is the Swan & Railway, Wigan, conveniently sandwiched between the town's two railway stations. It's also worth noting that railway travellers looked to stations to provide refreshments and at Stalybridge there is a rare example of an intact licensed station buffet from before the Second World War (famous as a real ale haven too!).

Between the Wars

The Great War brought pub-building to a full stop but it resumed fairly soon afterwards. The Carlisle area is famous for its inter-war pubs which were built as part of the State Management Scheme under its architect Harry Redfern (see pp. 34–5): sadly their interiors have nearly all been drastically changed. However, these pubs are emblematic of a shift from Victorian taste when ornate architecture and fittings had been in vogue. Now cleaner, simpler lines were usual, as at the Bridge, Rochdale, or in the harmonious neo-Georgian style of the Unicorn, Manchester. There was something of a Tudor revival too, exemplified by the Shakespeare, Farnworth, near Bolton, and an

Tudor styling was popular for pubs between the wars. This is the Shakespeare, Farnworth, near Bolton, of 1926

interest in half-timbering, as at a couple of Merseyside pubs, the Primrose, Liscard, and the Wheatsheaf, Sutton Leach. Out went ornate decoration – colourful ceramics (pp. 46–7) were a particular casualty – and in came large expanses of wall-panelling. Reducing

The interior of the Bleeding Wolf, Scholar Green, Cheshire, also looks back to the days of the Tudors (GB)

the number of pubs but improving standards in what remained had been the mission of magistrates for some years and continued the objectives of Victorian reformers. The bigger new pubs aimed at offering a respectable environment with a range of rooms and facilities to encourage a middle-class clientele and one that was increasingly mobile thanks to the motor car and yet to be troubled by drink-drive legislation! And not only men but women too (albeit in male company). Such pubs might also provide a green for bowling clubs, a garden and even a children's playground to encourage family visits.

After 1945

After the Second World War, Britain was bankrupt and hardly any pubs were built for a decade. The new ones that emerged in the mid-1950s were typified, not surprisingly for these straightened times, by utilitarian design and use of low-quality materials. Layouts, though, still provided a choice of rooms and almost always an off-sales facility for takeaway supplies. Needless to say, once the economy picked up, these cut-price reminders of the grey post-war years became highly unfashionable. Thus it is that intact post-war pubs are far rarer than Victorian ones. A couple of examples survive in Greater Manchester though: the Turnpike, Withington and the rather extraordinary Brindley Arms, Walkden. Curiously, the pretty much intact Queens Arms, Huyton, Merseyside, is securely dated to about 1958 but yet looks for all the world to belong to the 1930s.

Early post-war pub building was, necessarily, economically done. This is the Turnpike, Withington, Manchester (GB)

Characteristic *c.*1960 design at the Queens Arms, Huyton, Merseyside (1958) (GB)

The increased prosperity in the mid-1960s heralded a time of major change for the pub. The social divisions mirrored by the traditional multi-roomed pub were dissolving whilst magistrates and police favoured direct supervision of all public areas from the serving area – hence the widespread removal of internal walls to the great detriment of the atmosphere and attractiveness of traditional pubs. Other forces were at work too. The rise of off-licence shops and supermarkets during the 1960s made pub off-sales departments redundant. Environmental health officers demanded changes to accommodate inside toilets and better food

The rather extraordinary Brindley Arms, Walkden, Greater Manchester, built in the late 1950s. The public areas are single-storeyed: the three-storey part has accommodation above and a (former) off-sales below

Large inter-war pubs were often provided with extensive facilities, in this case a bowling green at the Nursery, Heaton Norris, Stockport (GB)

preparation facilities. Bar-back fittings were hacked about to make space for more varied and numerous products – wines, spirits, refrigerated drinks. Fire officers insisted on adaptations to provide safer escape routes. These relentless pressures resulted in a much-depleted pub heritage.

Modern times

Recent years have seen a tragic decline in the overall number of pubs in this country – down from around 70,000 in 1980 to less than 50,000 now. To some extent, this has been offset by the increase in bars, nearly all in town and city centres but, with some honourable exceptions, few of these have much merit in design terms and most will no doubt undergo a complete makeover every few years.

New pubs are still being built although conversions from existing buildings such as banks and shops are much more common. An encouraging trend has been the rise of the micro-pub, usually in a small redundant shop but they have no pretensions whatever to design excellence. It's noteworthy that in most years no winner can be found for the New Build category in CAMRA's annual Pub Design Awards – and also that at least two previous winners have subsequently been trashed and remodelled. On the other hand, public interest in our built heritage has never been higher, as evidenced by the numbers visiting National Trust and English Heritage properties. The very existence of this book and others published by CAMRA on pub heritage shows that this interest extends to pubs too. Sadly, we continue to lose historic pub interiors at an alarming rate. Mainly this is due to closures – down from an overall total peak of about 30 a week in early 2015 but still running at just over 20 – which affect heritage pubs like any others. And we still have owners with no appreciation for or interest in the often precious interiors of which they are custodians. The article on pages 15–16 looks at what can be done to help safeguard the treasures which survive.

What's Different about Pubs in the North West?

Like other Merseyside pubs, the Lion Tavern, Liverpool, has an L-shaped corridor wrapping round the public bar. They are much used, as here, by standing drinkers. Note the full-height screenwork

In the past four or five decades there has been a massive trend to open up pubs and pub builders today usually aim to have a single drinking space (look at most Wetherspoons, for example). A century or so ago it was very different and multiple rooms were the norm, as in the traditional pubs celebrated in this book. How these separate spaces were arranged varied enormously from pub to pub and it might seem to most pub goers that there is no geographical pattern. However, to take two very different examples, it's clear that Londoners were very keen on small, intimate screened-off compartments abutting the servery, the finest surviving example of which is the Prince Alfred, Maida Vale, W9, whereas in Northern Ireland there was a vogue for a line of snugs down the long wall facing the servery and separated from it by a wide space: the supreme example is the glorious Crown Bar in Belfast.

What of the North West? A common plan-form is to have a public bar on a street corner, surrounded by an **L-shaped corridor** which could be entered from either the main street and the side one.

King Edward VII, Guide, Lancashire. Rooms radiating off lobbies are often met with in north-west pubs

12

Full-height screens to the back of the servery at the Black Horse, Preston (GB)

Primrose, Liscard, Merseyside. Plan showing a wide opening between the lobby area and the smoke room on the left. The picture on p. 99 shows how it appears in reality (redrawn from Wirral Archive Services, ref. 79004: courtesy Historic England)

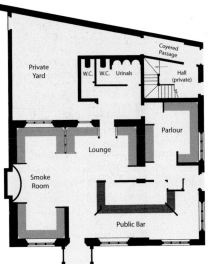

On the servery side of the corridor were tall screens. On the non-servery side there were further public rooms. These rooms were effectively the 'better class' rooms of the pub and tended to have upholstered seating and bell-pushes to attract table service (for which see p. 99). They might go under the names such as 'commercial room' or 'news room', pub room names which are unknown further south. There are several fine examples of these arrangements in this guide such as the Lion Tavern and Prince Arthur in Liverpool, the Stork Hotel, Birkenhead, and the Edinburgh, Crosby, Merseyside.

Another typical plan (which is also met with extensively on the other side of the Pennines) is to enter and find yourself directly in a relatively large space at the hub of the pub in front of the servery. In the guide we term this space a '**drinking lobby**'. The lobby area acted as the public bar and stand-up drinking was and is common there. Off this space various other rooms radiate. Instructive examples in this guide include the Victoria, Great Harwood, Lancashire, the Alexandra, Stockport, and Cemetery Hotel, Rochdale. And even the lobby bar of the mighty Philharmonic in Liverpool can be seen as a variant on this theme. An inter-war example is at the Whipping Stocks, Over Peover, Cheshire.

Associated with both these plan types are **glazed screens** which rise from the counter right up to the ceiling and house rising sashes to enable people to be supplied with drinks. Examples are also to be found in Yorkshire but they do seem to have been particularly popular in the North West. There are plenty of examples in this guide. Most have lost their sliding sashes but at the following all or some are still in working order: the Agricultural Hotel, Penrith, the Ship Hotel, Overton, Lancashire, the Lamb Hotel, Eccles, and, as a late, inter-war case, the Royal Oak in central Oldham. Many Holt's pubs were fitted out with them. For an especially ornate, Edwardian example visit the Springfield, Wigan, Greater Manchester.

Survey work by CAMRA has quite recently thrown up another regional speciality. We had always imagined that some of the **wide openings** off corridors and drinking lobbies were the result of modern opening up. However, many such openings are in fact 'historic' when examined closely. A case in point is the Primrose, Liscard, Merseyside, where such an opening is actually shown on a plan of 1922 (see also the photograph on p. 99). Other cases are to be found at the Crown, Birkenhead, Crows Nest, Crosby, Guest House, Southport, and Volunteer Canteen, Waterloo. All these are within Merseyside so this may be a localism in pub design of this area.

CAMRA and Pub Heritage

CAMRA was founded in 1971 to save Britain's traditional beer but it quickly became clear to campaigners that the best places to drink that beer, our pubs, were also under threat. In due course, CAMRA assigned equal importance to campaigning for real ale and for pubs.

From the 1970s there was a huge increase in the opening out of pubs and removals of fine fittings so preservation of historic pub interiors emerged as a key campaigning issue. After pioneering work in York in the late 1980s, a specialist Pub Preservation Group was set up, which evolved into today's Pub Heritage Group. The first step was to identify the most intact interiors surviving across the country's (then) 65,000 pubs. This massive task involved following up thousands of leads, developing criteria for inclusion, recording what was found (in words and photos) and creating a list – the National Inventory of Historic Pub Interiors (NI). At first this focused on interiors which remained largely unaltered since before the Second World War, though intact early post-war pubs were admitted later. Another development was to include pubs with specific features or rooms of real national significance.

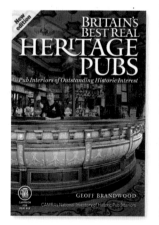

The first NI was published in 1997 and totalled 179 entries. Since then it has been continually refined and updated as new candidates were discovered and, sadly, existing entries lost. The present total stands at 278 and full descriptions can be found in our publication, *Britain's Best Real Heritage Pubs*, as well as on our website (see below).

Regional Inventories were the next logical step. As would be expected, the criteria for inclusion are set lower than for the NI though the same principles apply, with the emphasis on the internal fabric of the pub and what is authentically old. The selection criteria for both National and Regional Inventories are set out on page 123.

CAMRA also identifies a third category – pubs which have experienced still more change but which still have historic rooms or features felt to be of 'some regional importance'. These are included here as 'More to Try' at the end of each county section.

Inventory pubs in all three categories can be found on our website **www.heritagepubs.org.uk** where clicking on the Search Here facility in the top left-hand corner will take you to easy-to-use drop-down menus.

Pubs in Peril

Royal Oak, Eccles, Greater Manchester, a fine pub of 1904, but closed and under threat of alternative use at the time of writing (GB)

The current plight of the British pub is only too well known. At the time of going to press, figures show just over twenty closing each week and, between 1982 and 2017, total pub numbers fell by some 20,000. There are many reasons for this gloomy state of affairs – changing social habits, the smoking ban, the effect of the recession in the late 2000s, higher prices, the rapacious behaviour of the big pub companies. A particular threat is the attractiveness of many pub buildings to developers. Conversion of rural pubs to houses has been all too common for many years but it's now our urban pubs which are really suffering. Many suburban pubs, for instance, occupy large plots of land, ideal for small supermarkets, and two a week are being lost in that way alone. Such losses had been exacerbated by feeble planning laws which allowed the demolition of pubs and many changes of use without the need for planning permission. Strong campaigning by CAMRA and others led to these 'permitted development' rights being withdrawn in England in May 2017 so we hope the closure rate may now slow down. We are now campaigning for similar provisions to be enacted in the rest of the UK.

This combination of negative factors has posed major problems for urban heritage pubs. Many of them are to be found in unfashionable, off-centre locations where they ticked along for many years, serving the local community. As a result, their owners saw little point investing in the sort of major changes inflicted, in the pursuit of fashion, on many a town or city centre pub, so heritage was preserved, more or less by accident.

Sadly, though, when the recent recession began to bite, these pubs tended to drop the wrong side of the profits line. Historic pubs in peril can be, and have been, saved and CAMRA's Pub Heritage Group will fight for every one. One tactic is to draw a threatened pub to the

Listing in 1993 saved the Railway, Altrincham, Greater Manchester, from being demolished to make extra room for a retail development car park

attention of an enlightened small pub company and several pubs elsewhere in the country have been saved in just this way. We also seek to get pubs statutorily listed as this affords them an enhanced degree of protection (see below). Where we can, we use the planning system to resist unwanted changes to heritage pubs and encourage local folk to do likewise. Most of all, we aim to generate interest in these precious survivors. Pubs are first and foremost businesses and the more that people use them, the less likely are they to wither and die. You can do your bit by putting this guide to active use.

Statutory Listing

All parts of the United Kingdom and also the Isle of Man have systems for protecting buildings of special architectural or historic interest. Seventy-five of the 177 pubs in this guide are statutorily listed. The process is devised not to *prevent* change but to *manage* it effectively, working with the grain of the building, not against it.

In England, listings are made by the Secretary of State for Culture, Media and Sport, on the advice of Historic England. There are three grades:

Grade I. This highest of gradings covers just 2.5% of all listed buildings: these are those that have 'exceptional', even international interest.

Grade II* (spoken of as 'Two Star'). Covers a further 5.5% of listed buildings. They have 'outstanding' interest.

Grade II. 92% of listed buildings. They have what is described as 'special' architectural or historic interest.

In the Isle of Man the buildings are 'registered' (rather than 'listed') by the Manx Government's Department for Environment, Food and Agriculture. There is no grading system. Neither of the pubs in this guide are registered.

Cheshire

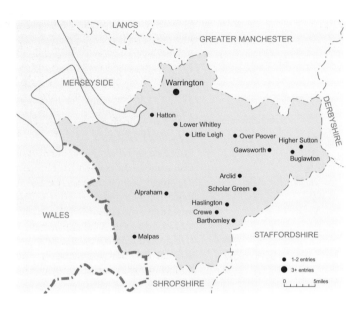

Alpraham

Chester Road, CW6 9JA

01829 260523

Not listed

LPA: Cheshire East

🍺 *Restricted opening hours*

Travellers Rest ★

A four-room wayside pub on the main road through the village. It once comprised just the T-plan building of around 1850 with its Tudor-style windows. This was extended, mainly at the back, in 1937, which is also the date of most of the (quite plain) fittings. Further changes took place around 1970 when the Wicker Room or Dart Room came into use.

Public bar

17

Back in the old part, the tap room (at the front) has a Victorian fireplace and 1930s mirror; a doorway leads to the tiny bar which is mostly the result of the 1937 refit. The lounge bar or 'New Room' was added at that time and retains its original fittings (but is normally only used when the bowling club meets). There is none of that new-fangled electronic gadgetry here – the till is a drawer in the bar counter and the likes of TVs, piped music and fruit machines are nowhere to be found. This pub has been in the hands of the same family for 110 years. The bowling green at the rear is still much used.

Arclid
Newcastle Road, CW11 2UG
01477 500332
www.legsofman.co.uk
Not listed
LPA: Cheshire East
🍺 🍴(L, E)

Entry on the left-hand side
is via a revolving door (GB)

Legs of Man ☆

Built in 1939 by architect J.H. Walters, this is one of the three major 1930s Cheshire roadhouses in this guide built for Robinsons Brewery (the others are the Church House, Buglawton, and Bleeding Wolf, Scholar Green). Unfortunately it lost its thatched roof to fire in 1956. The left-hand entrance retains its revolving door which leads into a large room which houses the servery with its original tapering bar counter (the bar-back is more recent). Note the Legs of Man over the fireplace. Archways have been cut to the room on the right which still has its original brick fireplace. A door on the right leads out to the gents' with four large original urinals and wall tiling. The restaurant (rear left) is much as it was originally with panelling and another Legs of Man over the fireplace. The gents' beyond the restaurant is also intact with two big urinals and tiled walls.

Barthomley
Audley Road, CW2 5PG
01270 882242
www.whitelionbarthomley.co.uk
Grade II* listed
LPA: Cheshire East
🍺 🍴(L)

White Lion ★

This fine half-timbered building, facing the medieval parish church, dates back to the early 17th century. The oldest part in terms of pub use is the delightful beamed tap room in the centre of the building. This never had a bar counter and drinks were brought from the parlour behind (now the kitchen). The furniture and fittings are from the 1930s, including a high-backed settle which appears to be constructed from reused old wall panelling. Note the glass-covered section of exposed wattle-and-daub on the left-hand side showing the method of filling in the walls between the timber framing. The fire surround is an unfortunate Modernist replacement of an inter-war brick one. The large room to the left (where the servery now is) has

Tap room, White Lion

seen use as a courtroom and a schoolroom before becoming part of the pub in 1953, which is the date of most of the fittings. The tiny room at the back was converted from private quarters in 1994.

Buglawton
Buxton Road, CW12 2DY
01260 272466
www.robinsonsbrewery.com/
churchhouse
Not listed
LPA: Cheshire East

 (L)

Church House ☆

One of three impressive multi-room roadhouses in this guide built for Robinsons in the 1930s in Cheshire under architect J.H. Walters (the others are the Legs of Man, Arclid, and Bleeding Wolf, Scholar Green). This one is said to have opened in 1941. Originally thatched like the Bleeding Wolf, the covering was lost to fire in June 1950. Much remains of the original layout. The public bar was on the left but was linked by an opening to the lounge in the early 1970s when a new lapped counter front was installed. On the far right is a smoke (now games) room with panelling and an attractive alcove. Right of the servery is a small drinking lobby which used to double as an off-sales. Note the sign 'Service' (and similar signs above the entrance to the gents' and the lounge doorways). The toilets off the corridor still have their original wall tiling and terrazzo floors. The rear room is very plain and was not originally in public use.

Games room (GB)

19

Crewe

140 Wistaston Road, CW2 7RQ
07912 796032
www.hoppolecrewe.co.uk
Not listed
LPA: Cheshire East

Hop Pole ☆

Rebuilt in the 1930s, and despite some erosion of layout and fittings, it is still a good example of a multi-room pub with a centrally placed, glazed servery rising from floor to ceiling. Sadly the rising sashes have gone and there are new counter fronts.

Lobby bar

However, the lobby bar is distinguished by an attractive quadrant-shaped counter. At the front right is the public bar with a red tiled floor and original fixed seating. The rear rooms have seen some opening up; each comes in two distinct parts. There are, however, survivals of original seating and remains of the bell-push arrangements. The fireplaces are modern replacements. There is still a functioning bowling green to the rear of the pub.

Gawsworth

Church Lane, SK11 9RR
01260 223325
www.robinsonsbrewery.com
Grade II listed
LPA: Cheshire East
 (L, E)

Harrington Arms ★

It is claimed there has been a pub here since 1710. Until 2007 it was attached to a working farm and thus was an example of a once-common way of combining pub-keeping with another livelihood. They are now separate businesses. The timeless tap room to the left of the entrance is the oldest part and has a red and black quarry-tiled floor, venerable settles, an old fireplace and sundry other vintage

furniture. The servery in its present form only dates from 1980. To the right, the snug has a hatch for service, a 1950s fireplace and a settle; the small lounge at the back has a similar period feel. The former kitchen on the rear left became part of the pub in 2007 (the former cooking facilities seem on a truly industrial scale, perhaps reflecting the need to provide food for farm workers). All the rooms have numbers on their doors.

Tap room

Haslington

137 Crewe Road, CW1 5RG
01270 582181
www.robinsonsbrewery.com
Grade II listed
LPA: Cheshire East
 (L)

The Oak Room is lined with
reused genuine historic panelling

Hawk Inn ★

The Hawk is a fine pub with a sequence of different rooms. These include the dining room on the left with an inter-war fireplace and old panelling. The Games Room (right) has a most interesting feature, an odd seat that projects out over the steps leading down to the cellar, and also a glazed section exposing the wattle and daub of its walling. But the star attraction is at the back of the pub. This is the Oak Room, lined with a rich display of old panelling, probably of early 17th-century origin and likely to have come from a gentry house, rather than an Armada galleon as the hoary old legend would have it. All this was there when Robinsons of Stockport bought the pub in 1929 from Kay's Atlas Brewery of Manchester. The room also has a Tudor-style stone fire-surround, 1920s fixed seating, bell-pushes and leaded windows. Over the fireplace are three decorative arches in relief, either side of which are paired columns.

Hatton

Hatton Lane, WA4 4DB
01925 730314
www.thehatton.co.uk
Grade II listed
LPA: Warrington
 (L, E)

Main bar

Hatton Bar & Grill (formerly Hatton Arms) ☆

A multi-room, early 19th-century pub which appears to have been refitted in the 1950s and is little changed since then. So many of the features appear to date from that time, notably the unusual (but typical of its time) counter of split logs, and also the bar-back, seating, fireplaces and faux half-timbering. The left door from the passage leads to the tap room in an extension to the original building. The former village post office and store on the right-hand end of the building has now been converted into a restaurant.

Higher Sutton

Sutton Lanes End, SK11 0NG
01260 400756
www.thehanginggate.co.uk
Not listed
LPA: Cheshire East
🍺 🍴 (L, E)

Hanging Gate ☆

This hillside pub is the highest in Cheshire and claims to date from 1621. It is included here for the two delightful, tiny left-hand rooms. A 1955 newspaper report details refurbishments to bring it 'up to standard' which probably included the counters we see today. The small middle bar has been enlarged by the removal of a side corridor. Off what remains of the corridor is a small parlour which has no real historic interest. In the late 1960s the cowshed was converted into a dining room and in 2006 further extended: from here are spectacular views over the open countryside. Gents' and ladies' are outside.

Left-hand bar (GB)

Little Leigh

Warrington Road, CW8 4QY
01606 853196
www.thehollybush.net
Grade II listed
LPA: Cheshire West & Chester
🍺 🍴 (L, E)

Holly Bush ☆

This timber-framed, thatched, three-room pub began life as a farmhouse. It was held for many years until 1999 by the same family and thus experienced little change. Then, in 2000, walling in the passage around the servery was removed and a small counter introduced for the first time. Previously drinks were fetched from the cellar. The front bar has a screeded floor, fixed benching, and a 1930s brick fireplace, almost inglenook in style. The two other small rooms retain an historic

Tap room

ambience. The front one has another 1930s brick fireplace plus post-war fixed seating and a disused front door. Up two steps is the snug, a small room with half-timbered walls which would have served as an overspill room in the past. The former living room at the rear right has been converted into a lounge and there is a new extension for a dining room. The outside gents' has been converted to the cellar and a new gents' (still outside) built.

Lower Whitley

Street Lane, WA4 4EN
01925 640044
www.chetwode-arms.co.uk
Grade II listed
LPA: Cheshire West & Chester
🍺 🍎 🍴 (E)
Closed
lunchtimes

Chetwode Arms ☆

A brown-brick village pub of around 1800 incorporating some earlier work. There are four old rooms, now increased to six. At the heart is a delightful small room right of the entrance with a panelled counter, probably inter-war, and with earlier glazed screenwork. Note the annunciator box over the doorway showing where table service was

required in days gone by. It names the parlour, tap room and dining room. On the right (not always open) is the small parlour with an inter-war panelled dado, a small serving hatch with sliding sashes, inter-war glazed brick coal fireplace, bench seating and two settles. At the rear is a cosy snug. On the front left is the dining room with an interesting old bench and glazed 1930s brick fireplace but a couple of holes have been cut into the upper parts of the wall 'for supervision'. Bowling green at the rear.

Hatch service
at the
Chetwode Arms

Malpas

Old Hall Street, SY14 8NE
01948 860368
Not listed
LPA: Cheshire West & Chester
🍺 🍎

Closed weekday lunchtimes

Red Lion ☆

A red-brick pub rebuilt in 1920 for the Northgate Brewery, Chester, and retaining many fittings from this time. The main bar, formerly consisting of two rooms, is at the front and retains the original bar counter and fixed seating. There are two further rooms at the rear. Noteworthy is some Jacobean panelling in the main bar which may have come from a previous inn on the same site. The pub is locally famous for possessing a three-legged chair which King James I is said to have used to watch a cockfight (currently located in the disused dining room on the right).

Public bar (GB)

23

Over Peover
Stocks Lane, WA16 8TU
01625 861455
Not listed
LPA: Cheshire East
 (L, E)

Park Gate Inn ☆

A brick-built village pub with no less than six small rooms which have extensive parquet flooring and inter-war fireplaces. The entrance lobby has seating on either side. A passage runs to the public bar in the heart of the pub (bar fittings replaced in the early 2000s). At the rear right is the small tap room with a red quarry-tiled floor and service via a very small, recently replaced counter. Left are two more small rooms, now linked by a wide gap. The front one has a partition wall to the passage: that at the rear contains settle seating. Right of the passage is the lounge, larger than the other rooms, with a couple of settles (the counter seems a recent replacement). Far right there is a door marked 'Private' but brought into use at busy times.

Public bar

Over Peover
Stocks Lane, WA16 9EX
01565 722332
Not listed
LPA: East Cheshire
 (L, E, not Mon)

Whipping Stocks Inn ☆

Although old-looking, this pub seems to have been rebuilt in the 1930s as a roadhouse (it used to be known as the Mainwaring Arms after the chief local family). There are four separate rooms off a spacious central bar where the bar counter front is of 1930s fielded panelling but the bar back is modern. There is a large inter-war brick fireplace with a shallow arch and coal fire. On the front left is a room that may have been two small ones in the past. The middle left room is small with another 1930s brick fireplace and settle-style fixed seating. The rear left 'Mainwaring Room' has fielded panelling to picture frame height, a largish 1930s brick fireplace and settle seating. On the front right is what locals call the 'Mourning Room' with a fine 1930s fireplace of brick and also beams.

Mainwaring Room

Scholar Green

121 Congleton Road North,
ST7 3BQ
01782 782272
www.thebleedingwolf.co.uk
Grade II listed
LPA: Cheshire East
 (L, E)

Bleeding Wolf ★

Architecturally impressive and remarkably intact, this pub was built in 1936 for Robinsons Brewery of Stockport under architect J.H. Walters. He employed what we might call a Roadhouse Vernacular Revival style which aimed for respectability and a nostalgic sense of history in the new motor age, an idea reinforced by the enormous thatched roof as an emblem of rustic tradition (see also the Legs of Man, Arclid on p. 18, and Church House, Buglawton on p. 19). The spreading plan of five rooms remains, along with most of the original fittings and finishes, notably the adzed tooling on the woodwork to suggest, once again, homely rusticity and hand craftsmanship. Facing the left-hand entrance is an off-sales hatch with the public bar on the left. To the right is a lounge which features the servery, an impressive inglenook fireplace and a lovely semi-circular bay at the front; note the depiction in stained glass of the bleeding wolf (whose legend is told in a panel on the wall). Further to the right is the dining room and to the rear left the fully panelled Oak Room – a splendid period piece. Finally, a former games room now houses the carvery. There is much original detailing throughout, for example, the delightful stained glass beer bottles either side of the entrance and original tiling in the toilets. Listed in 2011 following a successful application by CAMRA.

Main bar

Warrington

33 Church Street, WA1 2SX

07716 358945

Grade II listed

LPA: Warrington

Bulls Head ☆

Probably 17th-century – suggested by the date 1685 in a gable – this much restored inn is worth a visit for two small rooms of real character. Behind the servery an old latch door leads into a snug with two baffles/screens by the entrance with colourful stained glass panels, early 20th-century fixed seating, and bell-pushes around most of the room but, regrettably, a modern brick fireplace. Down a short passageway on the rear right a sliding door leads into the small Trophy Room with Victorian fixed seating with carved ends, and bell-pushes all around the room but, again, another modern brick fireplace. The rest of the pub is opened up and modernised but the area on the front right does retain old fixed seating and bell-pushes. There's an active bowling green at the back. Modern function room.

The snug

Warrington

175 Gorsey Lane, WA2 7RX

01925 240943

Grade II listed

LPA: Warrington

Orford Hotel ☆

A distinguished Tudor Gothic building with a stone-fronted, symmetrical façade built in 1908 for brewers Greenall Whitley. Much of the original six-room floor plan remains. On the right is the former 'Outdoor Department' (off-sales), named in etched glass. The public bar has its originally counter (slightly moved to the left), fixed seating but the tiled floor is new. A doorway leads to another room at the rear, served via a hatch. A passage down the rear has another hatch and a small alcove with seating. In the left-hand front door an etched glass panel announces 'Lounge Hall' and leads initially into a lobby bar (servery added in the 1970s but the fixed seating appears original). Art Nouveau tiling throughout the passageway. Both front and rear left-hand rooms have original seating (but fireplaces lost). The 'Lounge Hall' itself has plainer seating (perhaps inter-war work). The left-hand gents' is largely original (but with some painting over on the tiling unfortunately).

The right-hand bar, Orford Hotel, Warrington

Warrington

35 Tanners Lane, WA2 7NL
Not listed
LPA: Warrington

Three Pigeons ☆

A basic, multi-room, locals' pub with a public bar at the front containing old servery fittings and some unusual, perhaps 1920s, bentwood seating. The left-hand door leads to a passage and on this side are a couple of rooms, the front one with bell-pushes. At the rear right is now the pool room with old dado panelling and a fixed bench. The door from Lower Dallam Lane leads into a passage with a mosaic floor and the inner door has an etched panel advertising 'News Room'. The gents' has five original urinals and a separate WC with old dado tiling.

Public bar

MORE TO TRY

Here are seven pubs in Cheshire which are considered to have historic interiors of some regional importance.

Chester

Park Street, CH1 1RN
01244 340345
www.albioninnchester.co.uk
Not listed
LPA: Cheshire West & Chester
 ¶¶ (L, E)

Albion

The attractions here are the two right-hand rooms and double doors between them. The corner small bar has distinctive, possibly 1950s fittings while the small front right room has an early 20th-century fireplace and possibly 1950s seating. There were changes after Greenall Whitley bought the cottage on the left around 1980 and knocked down the dividing wall.

Crewe

56 Earle Street, CW1 2AT
Not listed
LPA: Cheshire East

Kings Arms

A four-room pub with a variety of inter-war fittings. Examples of these are the inter-war seating and wall-panelling in various parts, largely intact gents', and the etched 'Games Room' panel in the door glazing. Off the Rainbow Street entrance is a very pleasing vestibule with fixed bench seating. The rear right snug has service bells and an inter-war wood-surround fireplace (but modern infill). A recent refurbishment has covered many of the surfaces with pastel blue paint which has greatly altered the character of the pub.

Hoole

16 Faulkner Street, CH2 3BD
01244 401620
Not listed
LPA: Cheshire West & Chester

Royal Oak

A simple, three-room Victorian end-of-terrace pub with various inter-war fittings. The panelled corridor leads to the rear where the servery (with modern changes) is on the left. There is fixed seating in place and the gents' (advertised in 1930s etched glass) is pretty much intact with three big urinals (but wall-tiles, sadly, painted over). On the front right a doorway leads to a small room with a bagatelle table, a rare pub game only seen in the Chester area and in Coventry.

Lower Stretton

Northwich Road, WA4 4NZ
Not listed
LPA: Warrington

Closed lunchtimes

Ring o' Bells

The layout of two tiny rooms on the left and the bar on the right was last changed in 1965 when the bar was extended to the right into a former private lounge. Part of the old partition wall to the tiny front left room remains and forms two high backed settles with iron rods fixed to ceiling, and there is a pewter bar top on the hatch to the side of the bar. Fixed seating is at least forty years old, bar counter, bar back and one fireplace date from 1930s.

Front snug at the Ring o'Bells

Mobberley

Knolls Green, WA16 7BW
01565 873149
Not listed
LPA: Cheshire East
 (L, E)

Bird in Hand

This 18th-century pub retains three snugs at the front and lots of 1930s fittings. That on the left has a lino floor, panelled dado, brick fireplace and two small old benches. The second snug has old fixed benches. The third has an arch, benches, Victorian-style fireplace with log fire and a baffle at one end of the seating. At the rear right the gents' retains intact 1930s work including three big urinals.

Smallwood

Spen Green, CW11 2XA
01477 500262
www.bluebellsmallwood.co.uk
Not listed
LPA: Cheshire East
 (L, E)

Blue Bell

Said to have doubled as farmstead and alehouse as far back as 1727. The pub core consists of a couple of tiny rooms in the centre with large, exposed structural timbers. They now have lapped bar counters whose date is hard to determine (anywhere from the 1930s to the 1970s). Expansion then took place left and right and all four front spaces are now linked by a passage. The toilets (right) seem inter-war. Finally a large but quite sensitive addition for dining was built on the left-hand side in 2011.

Wilmslow

71 Chapel Lane, SK9 5JH
01625 532443
Not listed
LPA: Cheshire East

Farmers Arms

A busy locals' pub, built in the early 20th century, but refitted in the 1930s with further subsequent changes. The small vault has an old counter and bench seating but the bar-back seems to be of the 1960s. At the rear is another small room with old bench seating and a fireplace that could date from the 1930s. On the right are two more small rooms: a large piece of wall above the dado was removed in the early 2000s. The rear room was a private living room until the early 1980s. The front lounge bar has what may be a 1950s counter, 1960/1970s fixed seating and a new fireplace. The games room upstairs has been brought into use. Two old urinals in the gents'. Modern window glass.

29

Rooms in Historic Pubs

Until the late 20th century pubs almost invariably consisted of two or more public rooms. They went under a wide variety of names, the meaning of which was often quite fluid. Some of the names are regional as we shall see. The quality of the surroundings on offer varied from room to room and with this went differentials in pricing. You paid less for your beer in the public bar which was the most simply appointed and often very much the domain of the working man. Here there would be a bar counter, no carpet on the floor, lots of smoke in the air, and the standard drink would be mild (which has now all but disappeared from our pubs). In the north of England a common alternative name for the public bar was the vault.

Better-appointed rooms went under a variety of names. The lounge and saloon (sometimes lounge saloon) tended to be larger and one might expect carpets, panelling and service at your table (see p. 119). Much the same might be expected in the smoke/smoking room. These latter names are a little puzzling since there was no restriction on smoking throughout a pub. Maybe the idea was to suggest somewhere where people could take their ease in the way they would have done in a smoking room of a gentleman's residence? Then there were club rooms, function rooms, music or concert rooms, billiard rooms and off-sales compartments (p. 52), for all of which the purpose is self-evident.

'Vault' is a common alternative name for 'public bar' in the North West (GB)

A step up from the vault/public bar; the smoke room (GB)

In the North West one sometimes comes across commercial and news rooms where customers might do business or relax for a quiet read. The snug, a name found throughout most of the UK and still widely used, was, as the name suggests, generally a smallish, cosy space. Parlour or bar parlour

The news room, another North West speciality, would no doubt have had a similar atmosphere to a commercial room

was a popular North-West name for what is often called a lounge elsewhere. One puzzling name is the tap room. One might be forgiven for thinking that this was where drinks were dispensed but examination of old plans of pubs, and the evidence from ones where tap rooms exist shows this was not the case in the vast majority of instances because the room was separated from, and often at a fair distance from, the servery. One long-serving licensee has suggested that in tap rooms regulars would tap a coin or their glass to attract attention to summon service. Well, maybe!

The commercial room, a popular name in the North West, at the Shakespeare, Farnworth, near Bolton. Today it looks no different from other rooms but in the past would probably have been rather more tranquil than the vault/public bar

Cumbria

SCOTLAND

NORTHUMBERLAND

● Carlisle

● Bassenthwaite Lake

COUNTY DURHAM

● Howton

● Great Langdale

● Kendal

● Broughton Mills

NORTH YORKSHIRE

LANCASHIRE

● 1-2 entries

0   5miles

Bassenthwaite Lake
CA13 9YE (South off A66,
west end of lake)
017687 76234
www.the-pheasant.co.uk
Not listed
LPA: Allerdale
 (L, E) ⛏

Pheasant Inn ★

The atmospheric public bar of this fine old Georgian coaching
inn has not changed in many years. It is divided into two parts by
a wide, shallow arch. The layout comprises a relatively small area
in front of the counter and, behind the arch, a somewhat larger
space for drinkers and diners. Positioned within the north side of
the arch is a wondrously old gas fire. There is much panelling and
the whole place would have been recognisable to Lakeland tourists
of past generations. Elsewhere, a lounge bar (residents only) has
some 1930s features and, in the side passage, there is a two-part
glazed hatch inscribed 'Waiters Only', plus two old glazed panels.

Public bar, Pheasant Inn,
Bassenthwaite Lake

Broughton Mills
LA20 6AX
01229 716824
www.theblacksmithsarms.com
Grade II listed
LPA: South Lakeland

The rustic-looking left-hand room

Blacksmiths Arms ★

Floored throughout with stone flags, the Blacksmiths, albeit in a gentrified state with a strong emphasis on dining, offers an impression of how an old Lakeland country inn might have been. The original bar was on the right and had no bar counter until 1996. The room to the left is of much more interest and is divided from the passageway by a solid wooden screen with benches attached. It contains a cast-iron range (hence its name of the 'Range Room') and a fitted cupboard of the former kitchen, showing how the public house developed out of a private one. In more recent times the pub has expanded into the former shop (rear right) and living accommodation (far left).

Carlisle, centre

22 Botchergate, CA1 1QS
01228 536900
www.thecumberlandinn.co.uk
Grade II listed
LPA: Carlisle

Cumberland Inn ☆

The least-altered of the pubs built under the Carlisle State Management Scheme and its architect Harry Redfern. It dates from 1929–30 and is a good example of his high quality designs, in this case in the Tudor Revival style on a long, narrow site and costing a hefty £13,678. There has been a fair amount of opening out and refitting but a strong sense of the intended elegant ambience can

still be felt, evoked in particular by the fielded panelling and stone fireplaces. Upstairs, two formerly little-used bars now house a separate business, the Royal Outpost Restaurant, accessed by a staircase from the right-hand door. Both rooms have original bar fittings, excellent fireplaces and panelled walls with gilded inscriptions in praise of moderate drinking. Above the panelling are painted cartouches and vine motifs with jugs and glasses over the fireplaces.

The panelled front room

Carlisle, Etterby

Kingmoor Road, CA3 9RS
01228 527253
Grade II listed
LPA: Carlisle

🍺 🍴 (L, E)

Redfern Inn ☆

Built for the State Management Scheme and opened on 1 October 1940. It was named in honour of Harry Redfern (1861–1950), the Scheme's architect from 1916, and was designed in Arts & Crafts style by his assistant Joseph Seddon (with Redfern's collaboration). Since then, the counter in the public bar has been extended and there has

been much wall removal between the right-hand front room and that behind (originally known as a 'tea and smoking room'). Some fireplaces have also been replaced. However, much wooden panelling survives along with a wealth of detail, such as the door furniture, so there is still much to cherish here. The bowling green has been out of use for a number of years and is under threat from development.

The former tea room and smoking room

The 'Carlisle Experiment'

For over fifty years the Carlisle district was used by the Government as a test-bed for the theory that excessive alcohol consumption could be controlled and reduced through the design of the places where drink was sold and enjoyed.

Alcohol was the subject of serious debate in late Victorian and Edwardian Britain, with social campaigners concerned about its harmful impact on society who were pitted against a large and profitable drinks industry. During the First World War, drink, and its potential impact on the war effort, became a major concern. In June 1915 the Central Control Board (Liquor Traffic) was set up to regulate the production, sale and consumption of alcohol. As the war progressed, opening times for pubs were seriously reduced, the strength of beer was progressively lowered, and its supply rationed.

Furthermore the Central Control Board gained powers to control the sale of alcohol where national security required it. Nowhere was the Government more concerned about the effect that drink had on the war effort than in an area centred on Carlisle. North of the city and into southern Scotland lay the vast National Munitions Factory, where thousands of workers, many of them women, produced the shells fired by the army and the navy. The site also employed thousands of navvies to construct many new buildings so that production could be expanded. It was these men who descended on Carlisle at the weekends in search of drink, and gave the city an unrivalled reputation for drunkenness and disorder. In the first six months of 1916 Carlisle had a higher rate of drink-related convictions than any other town in England.

The Government authorised the Central Control Board to take control of the sale of drink around the National Munitions Factory.

The **Redfern Inn**, Etterby, Carlisle: opened 1940 and named after the architect to the Carlisle State Management Scheme

ANDREW DAVISON

Upstairs at the **Cumberland Inn**, Carlisle, elegantly built and fitted out in 1929–30

In July 1916 pubs and off-licences in Carlisle, Gretna and the surrounding area were purchased by the Board. The English part, stretching from the Scottish border to Maryport, contained 339 licensed premises, as well as a number of breweries, all of which except the Old Brewery in Carlisle were immediately closed.

The Board then moved quickly to close the smaller and more disreputable pubs – by the end of 1917, fifty-three had been closed – and also set about enhancing the facilities in those that remained. Even as the war continued, new 'improved' pubs were opened, the first two by the end of 1916. A programme of reconstructing existing pubs was also begun.

At the end of the war, the decision was taken to retain state control of what was now known as the Carlisle State Management Scheme, run by the Home Office. New pubs were built, intended to act as models for those elsewhere. Their design was in the hands of the Scheme's architect, Harry Redfern. All had a variety of rooms, large numbers of seats and tables, a short bar counter (to dissuade people from standing-up drinking) and well-equipped kitchens, to ensure that food and hot drinks could be served. Many of the suburban and country pubs had bowling greens, another way of distracting patrons from drinking. Most were in a pleasant Arts and Crafts style,

although some of the city centre pubs had more unusual designs.

After the Second World War, and Redfern's retirement, new pubs continued to be built, their design reflecting changing fashions in architecture. The Scheme had been seen as a model for potential state control of the drink industry, but by 1971 nationalisation was no longer on the political agenda, and the Scheme was abolished. By 1973 the pubs had been sold to a variety of new owners. The Old Brewery was bought by Theakston's of Masham, a small Yorkshire brewery struggling to keep up with the demand for their ales created by support from a new drinkers' organisation – CAMRA.

Great Langdale

LA22 9JY

015394 37272

www.odg.co.uk

Not listed

LPA: South Lakeland

Old Dungeon Ghyll Hotel ☆

At the side of this secluded hotel in the Langdale Valley sits the 'Hikers' Bar', converted from a shippon (cow-shed) in 1949 and hardly changed since. Two stalls, made from timber and white-painted slate, were retained to provide characterful drinking booths; they also divide the barn-like interior. On the left-hand side, a massive cast-iron open fire burns all year round, a welcome sight for cold and thirsty walkers, some of whom have left carved messages in the simple wooden tables. The right-hand part has more utilitarian features. The long bar counter is faced with white-painted slate plus plentiful timbering. The linoleum floor conceals a slate original. Although very simply appointed, the bar has great atmosphere.

* The left-hand area

Howtown

CA10 2ND,

01768 486514

www.howtown-hotel.co.uk

Not listed

LPA: Eden

Howtown Hotel ☆

Arguably, the highlight of a stay at this charmingly old-fashioned hotel overlooking Ullswater is being able to use the Residents' Bar, though casual visitors are generally welcome to take a peek as well.

Residents' bar

The small room is formed by a leaded partition/screen with rising lower sections. It has a panelled, possibly Victorian, counter, an old bar-back with slender columns supporting the shelves, inter-war fireplace, antique settle and an ancient till which takes several rings to record each transaction. The public bar at the back is also small, with a modern quarry-tiled floor, panelled dado, a hatch-like counter and a variety of furniture, including more old settles. Toilets (modernised) for both sexes are outside. You can get here on an Ullswater 'steamer'.

Kendal

39 Kirkland, LA9 5AF
01539 720326
www.ringobellskendal.webs.com
Grade II listed
LPA: South Lakeland
 (L)

The tiled corridor and entrance to the tiny snug

Ring o' Bells ☆

Dating from the early 18th century, this is reputedly the only pub in England built on consecrated ground (it is adjacent to the parish church). The lobby retains its off-sales hatch and a portion of Victorian bench seating whilst the bar on the left has a screened counter with two tiers of stained glass panels. It also has half-height panelled walls, an inter-war fireplace and a well-worn Formica-topped card table. Next is a tiny snug, also panelled and with old bench seating. There's yet more panelling in the lounge at the back and another 1920s fireplace but the counter and seating are modern. The small dining room beyond came into use only recently.

MORE TO TRY

Here are four pubs in Cumbria which are considered to have historic interiors of some regional importance.

Carlisle, Currock

Boundary Road, CA2 4HH
Not listed
LPA: Carlisle

Currock

This large Victorian pub still has three rooms, including the last-surviving billiard room functioning in Carlisle with its two full-sized tables. The public bar has its Victorian counter (now painted purple!), old dado panelling but a modern bar-back and seating. The lounge was formerly two small rooms and retains original fixed seating and an old fireplace. This is almost certainly the last pub in the country where you can play the game of table bowls, once popular in this area (although it is still played in many of the city's clubs and there are three leagues). It is a miniature version of the outdoor game with similarly biased balls which are rolled from a chute.

Agricultural Hotel

Penrith
Castlegate, CA11 7JE
01768 862622
www.jenningsbrewery.co.uk/
pubs
Not listed
LPA: Eden
 (L, E)

This ivy-covered hotel built of local sandstone in 1807 is well worth a visit to see one of the finest surviving Victorian shuttered and panelled serveries. It still has working sash screens which reach right up to the ceiling. It is two-sided, of three bays length, two bays on the return, and a curved bay at the corner. The five main bays have lower sliding screens with the corner bay and upper ones having fixed glazed panels. The bar-back fitting is mainly old with some wood and modern colourful stained glass. Sadly in the late 1990s there was a major refurbishment that opened up the pub.

Dockray Hall

Penrith
Great Dockray, CA11 7DE
01768 210676
https://dockrayhall.com
Grade I listed
LPA: Eden
 (L, E)

A wonderful building dating back to the 15th century when it was reputedly home to Richard, Duke of Gloucester, later Richard III, but much altered in the 16th century. It became an inn in 1719. The 'Main Bar' retains, in its raised area, lots of 16th-century panelling and a 17th-century stone fireplace. In the lower area, there is a large stone fireplace: the bar-back is very modern but the counter was created perhaps in the 1930s and includes reused work from a couple of bed headboards. On the left is the 'Old Bar' with a massive inglenook fireplace, beamed ceiling and old panelling. The bar counter may be forty or so years old (but new top) but the bar-back is definitely modern. Various rear rooms, but with no old fittings. After a period of closure it reopened in July 2016 after a careful restoration.

Masons Arms

Strawberry Bank
Bowland Bridge, LA11 6NW
01539 568486
www.masonsarmsstrawberry
bank.co.uk/masons
Not listed
LPA: South Lakeland
 (L, E)

The present layout was created in the late 1950s or early '60s when the counter was re-positioned further back from the front door and re-fronted (the modern marble top added in recent years). At this time part of the wall was removed so the front left room is nearly opened up to that on the right and which has a flagstone floor, range and settles. Beyond is a small bare wooden floored room with a narrow door and fixed seating. The rear right area with its kitchen range was brought into use in the 1950/'60s and has been extended to the rear. Four small upstairs rooms are now in use for dining.

Lancashire

Bacup
12 Yorkshire Street, OL13 9AE
01706 876183
Not listed
LPA: Rossendale

Little Queens (formerly Queens Hotel) ☆

Despite considerable opening out and alteration at the back, there remains much to enjoy at the front. A tiled passage leads to a lobby bar where a small surviving section of the counter sports green Art Nouveau tiles. The authentically traditional tap room, front left, has a wood block floor, fixed seating all round, bell pushes, old fireplace and narrow scrubbed tables. Front right, the snug (now the pool room) has lost its fixed seating but other features like the parquet floor and fireplace are of a good age. Tiling continues up the stairs and in the passage to the toilets – most of the stained and leaded glass is, however, modern.

In the snug

39

Blackpool, centre
204 Talbot Road, FY1 3AZ
01253 749196
Not listed
LPA: Blackpool

Ramsden Arms Hotel ('The Rammy') ☆

An imposing 'Brewers' Tudor' pub, built in 1939 for Thomas Ramsden's of Halifax. The main bar has panelled walls to picture-rail height, a Tudor-style fireplace and old fixed seating; the bar counter has a recent top and the bar-back is a modern replacement. Two small rooms at the front still have their brick fireplaces and fixed seating

but have been opened up to the main bar. One displays marquetry panels with hunting scenes which reputedly came from the predecessor pub, demolished for road widening. The bar to the right was once two small rooms but again has some old fittings of quality. The gents' on the left, with five big urinals, is splendidly intact.

Left-hand snug

Blackpool, Marton
286 Whitegate Drive, FY3 9PH
01253 767827
www.thesaddleblackpool.co.uk
Not listed
LPA: Blackpool

Saddle Inn ☆

The area entered from the hallway has seen much change in recent years, with a former men-only snug now incorporated into the lobby and only some of the fittings hanging on, including the bar counter with remnants of sliding sashes. The two rooms to the right, though, have much to commend them. The first has matchboarded walls, ceilings finished in Lincrusta, brass bell-pushes, fitted seating and a stained glass panel above the door. In the other is more Lincrusta, more bell-pushes and matchboarded walls. A rear extension accommodates a food servery. It is said to have been licensed since 1776.

An inviting snug at the Saddle

Chorley
38 Hollinshead Street, PR7 1EP
01257 266401
Not listed
LPA: Chorley

Trader Jack's ☆

Although much altered, this pub retains much of the typical north-western layout (pp. 12–13) of a passage round the servery, with several rooms off and a small corner public bar. The counter for the latter is Victorian but the pot-shelves are modern. On the Clifford Street side, a small, plainly furnished room is separated from the passageway by a tall, glazed partition. Off the corner of the lobby is another small room with old seating but more recent panelling. A further room, rear left, has old panelling while the room on the right has been opened up to the lobby. Throughout the pub a number of holes have been cut into walls and windows inserted to aid 'supervision'.

One of the snugs

Clayton-le-Moors
13 Church Street, BB5 5HT
01254 871506
Not listed
LPA: Hyndburn
 (breakfasts)

Old England Forever ☆

The little-altered Edwardian public bar is the star feature at this drinkers' pub which is set in a terrace of houses. It has a red quarry-tiled floor with chequerboard edging, an old bar counter and bar-back (though the counter top may be new), fixed seating and dado panelling. It is reached through a fully tiled entrance porch and a door with an etched panel declaring 'smoke room'. On the left, two small rooms were knocked into one in the mid-1990s. However, the panelling and seating seem old: service is via a hatch. The small games room at the back can be accessed from both of the other rooms and also has a servery hatch.

Public bar

41

Cleveleys

183 Victoria Road West, FY5 3PZ

01253 853306

Not listed

LPA: Blackpool

The vast left-hand room.
The partitioned seating is modern

Victoria ☆

A mighty inter-war edifice, built to cater both for visitors and a large middle-class estate. The heavy timber-work in the huge lounge imparts a quasi-baronial feel and everything else, including the original bar counter and Tudor-style stone fireplaces, is on the same scale. Internal screens now create seating areas to break up the cavernous space. A plain snug to the side has stained and leaded windows but nothing else of interest. The public bar also has its original counter and bar back whilst the corridor sports an Art Deco terrazzo floor and tiling to two-thirds height. The off-sales is still *in situ* but unused.

Darwen

25 Chapels, BB3 0EE

01254 702510

Not listed

LPA: Blackburn & Darwen

Punch Hotel ☆

A Victorian red-brick locals' pub which, remarkably, still has five separate rooms plus a lobby bar. The tiling in the entrance lobby has been painted over: beneath the carpet is a mosaic with the name of the pub. A refit during the 1960s resulted in much Formica adorning bar counters and bar-backs and the loss of some fireplaces but nothing much has changed since then. Original features include the terrazzo floors in the entrance and lobby bar, a parquet floor in the 'Dog House' and fixed seating in several rooms. The room at the back, with its old wall cupboards, was formerly in domestic use. Three rooms have pool tables and another a small snooker table. The gents' toilets retain the original three big urinals.

The simply-appointed snug

Goosnargh

Horns Lane, PR3 2FJ
01772 865230
www.yehornsinn.co.uk
Grade II listed
LPA: Preston

 (L, E)

Horns Inn ★

This rather isolated, hard-to-find pub has long been a wayside inn. A stone outside is dated 1782 but the structure may well be older. The interior was last significantly changed in the mid-1950s when a partition was removed from between the public bar and a corridor to create what is now the main bar in front of the servery (its brick frontage is probably interwar). The counter still has its functioning sliding screens. However, the star feature is the area behind it, where customers and serving staff actually co-exist in the same space. The door into it is marked 'Private' so as a courtesy ask if it is possible to sit there (it generally is). The only other known surviving examples of this rare arrangement are at the Bridge Inn, Topsham, Devon, and the Arden Arms, Stockport (p. 76). This small room has a baffle at the entrance, a brick and wood fireplace, old shelving, a panelled dado and a carved settle. There are some good features elsewhere, notably the fine plasterwork to the small dining room ceiling. On-site brewing began in March 2013.

The public drinking space
behind the servery

Great Harwood

St John's Street, BB6 7EP
01254 885210
Grade II listed
LPA: Hyndburn

Victoria ('Butcher Brig') ★

This superb Edwardian pub of 1905 provides a friendly environment for a drink, with many quality ales on offer. The lobby bar, passageway and staircase all have full-height cream and green tiling with flower motifs. The counter too has a tiled front and also working screens. All the ceilings are wood-panelled. Four small rooms lead off the lobby, mostly with original fittings. Three are named in the door glass – the Commercial Room (with notable Art Nouveau fireplace), the Bar Parlour (another fine fireplace), another parlour, and the 'Public Kitchen'. This latter name, probably now unique in a pub, may recall how some pubs offered cooking and food heating facilities to the poor.

At the end of the passage is a fifth room, recently converted to pub use. Above the staircase is a splendid stained glass window. The only altered area is to the right of the entrance, where the door opening has been widened. Originally, there was a 'Jug Department' here with hatch service, and its door has been re-sited to the ladies' toilet (likewise the smoke room door to the gents'). The nickname comes from a long-gone slaughterhouse and railway bridge. The former bowling green now forms part of the extensive beer garden. Listed in 1997 following a pilot study of Lancashire pubs by CAMRA for English Heritage.

The tiled and screened servery, Victoria, Great Harwood

Guide

321 Haslingden Road, BB1 2NG

01254 54261

Not listed

LPA: Blackburn & Darwen

King Edward VII ☆

Originally the Guide Inn but rebuilt in Edwardian times (hence the name), this pub retains many cut-glass windows and decorative wall-tiling plus attractive friezes on the walls of two lobbies, around the rear bar area and up the staircase to the former function room. The front right-hand room is somewhat opened out but still has original fixed seating and an impressive fireplace with a fine mirrored-surround mantlepiece. The room rear right also retains its fixed seating but the fireplace has gone. The same features can be found in the rear left room but here the inglenook fireplace survives (the servery hatch seems a later addition). The bar fittings are from the 1960s or 1970s as is the seating in the front left area.

The tiled passage with rooms leading off

Haskayne

1 Delph Lane

Downholland, L39 7JJ

01704 840033   Not listed

LPA: West Lancashire

Kings Arms ☆

The two small right-hand rooms are the main interest here, refitted in the 1930s, with their dado panelling, fixed seating and parquet floors. The counter is from the same era but the bar-back is recent and the fireplace partly modern. In the rear room, the panelling above the (modern) fireplace seems of the 1930s and has three painted sections portraying kings and queens. The front and side rooms feature lots of good 1930s stained glass windows and dado panelling runs up a staircase leading to the now closed lounge bar. The left bar was extended in recent years to incorporate former living space but the front counter may be old and the fixed seating at the front certainly is.

On the Tiles – Architectural Ceramics in Pubs

One of the glories of late Victorian and Edwardian pubs is the use of ceramics and this guide draws attention to examples in the region. As early as 1850 the billiard room at Gurton's in Old Bond Street, London, was decorated with pictorial ceramic panels, but it is unlikely that such work was common until the 1880s. Thereafter ceramics were employed in various forms, ranging from their mundane, but, very necessary, use in toilets, through floor and wall tiling, to rich mosaic flooring, pictorial panels, and even ceramic bar counters. Tiles were more expensive than wood but had the great advantage of being hard-wearing and – useful in the smoky atmosphere of the pub in bygone days – hygienic, as they were easily cleaned. The golden age of pub ceramics was between the 1880s and the First World War. For an easily visitable ceramic wonderland go to the Marble Arch Inn, Manchester (p. 64), dating back to 1888, where the walls,

floor and even the ceiling are so-treated.

The most exotic use of ceramics is for solid blocks facing **bar counters** and the North West has four examples of such work (technically known as faience) out of fifteen in England. The grandest – indeed in the entire country – is in St Anne's-on-Sea at Burlingtons Bar, facing the station. The wonderful, fully-tiled room housing it is closed at the time of going to press (but viewable through the windows or on request at the pub above). A close runner-up is in the public bar at the Black Horse, Preston, which provides a real master-class in pub ceramics. The other examples are at the Hark to Towler, Tottington, in Greater Manchester, and the Castle, Manchester. In addition, more simple, tiled counter fronts are to be found at the Prince Arthur, Liverpool; Queens, Bacup, the Victoria, Great Harwood, and the Crooked Billet, Worsthorne, all in Lancashire; and Royds Arms, Rochdale and White Lion,

The public bar, **Black Horse**, Preston, 1898 (

Westhoughton (the last probably from the 1920s), both in Greater Manchester. As well as its many other splendours, the Philharmonic Dining Rooms in Liverpool even has a counter faced with mosaic.

Another exotic use of ceramics in vogue between the 1880s and the First World War was for pictorial **tiled paintings**. They are mostly in otherwise altered pubs, the one exception in this guide being the Flower of the Valley, Rochdale, where a lovely panel by the entrance shows a stylised, Art Nouveau lily of the valley. Rochdale has quite a concentration of tiled paintings in pubs. Other examples (not in this guide) are four at the Brown Cow, Edenfield Road in the Norden area; entrance lobby ones at the Waggon & Horses, 366 Manchester Road; Nelson Hotel, 131 Drake Street; and the Eagle Hotel, 59 Oldham Road.

Enterprising ceramic work sometimes found a place in **fireplaces**

Lobby bar, White Lion, Westhoughton, Greater Manchester

Windsor Castle, on Craven Dunnill tiles, comes to the Brown Cow, Norden, Rochdale

Ceramics everywhere – Burlington's Bar, St Anne's-on-Sea, Lancashire. Craven Dunnill provided an identically detailed counter for the great Crown Bar in Belfast (GB)

Three examples of note are at the Crown Hotel and the Globe in central Liverpool and the suburb of Toxteth, respectively, and the Black Horse, Preston.

Tiled dados were widely employed and there are numerous examples in this guide. A couple of especially good examples are at the Alexandra, Stockport, and the Cemetery Hotel, Rochdale. Others can be found at the Stanley Arms, Eccles, the Bridge, Horwich, and White Lion, Hyde, all in Greater Manchester: in central Manchester itself they occur at the Briton's Protection, Hare & Hounds and Mr Thomas's Chop House. Occasionally walls could be tiled right up to the ceiling as at the King Edward VII, Guide, and the Victoria, Great Harwood, both Lancashire.

Mosaic was widely used for the floors of entrance lobbies, often stating the name of the pub in question. Mosaic might also be used for the flooring of corridors, drinking lobbies or a particular bar. Fine examples are at the Black Horse, Preston; Alexandra, Stockport; Stork, Birkenhead, and the Lion Tavern, Boundary, Edge Hill and Prince Arthur, Walton, all in Liverpool.

Advertising floor mosaic at the Perch Rock, New Brighton, Merseyside (not in this guide)

Fireplace in the front bar at the Crown Hotel, Liverpool, c.1905 (GB)

Green tiles were popular for dados in pubs. This particularly rich example is at the Cemetery Hotel, Rochdale, Greater Manchester (GB)

Nether Kellett

32 Main Road, LA6 1EP
Not listed
LPA: Lancaster

🍺 *Restricted opening hours*

Overton

9 Main Street, LA3 3HD
07979 030196
Not listed
LPA: Lancaster

🍺 Closed Mon and Tue

Landlady Stephanie Province raises
the glazed sashes on the servery

Limeburners Arms ☆

A plain, early 19th-century building which is still part of a working farm. It's been in the same family hands since 1931. There is a simple public bar with old fittings, including a shuttered counter with a glazed screen (though the sashes are now raised permanently). In recent years the staircase was removed and the bar expanded on the right-hand side where the domino table now stands. The small right-hand room has always been even plainer in comparison. The present owner has cut a gap in the rear wall to create a walkway to the servery. Outside toilets. Beer is sometimes dispensed by means of a cask pump, a very rare arrangement nowadays. Closed Mon, opens 7.45 Tue–Sat, 4 Sun.

A very rare method of dispense: a cask pump in action

Ship Hotel ☆

The pub occupies a couple of cottages and served as a hotel for Victorian and early 20th-century tourists. The star feature is a shuttered servery (cf. the Agricultural Hotel, Penrith) in the main bar. It has three bays and, like the Penrith example, the sliding sashes are still in full working order. They were presumably lowered when time was called. Two rooms have Victorian coloured tile floors. That in the main bar shows how there must have been a screen and door between the entrance and the bar. The other tiled floor is in the games room (far left). The pub was kept from 1934 to 1976 by Mrs 'Ma' Macluskie and the upstairs function room is named in her honour. There you can see an amazing display of birds' eggs for which the pub was long famous (originally displayed on the ground floor). The pub reopened in March 2016 after what seemed permanent closure and has been lovingly restored.

Preston

166 Friargate PR1 2EJ
01772 204855
Grade II listed
LPA: Preston

  (L)

Late Victorian ceramic riches
in the public bar

Black Horse ★

This is a wonderfully impressive pub from the great days of Victorian urban pub-building and doubled as a small hotel. It was rebuilt in 1898 to designs of local architect J. A. Seward for Kay's Atlas Brewery of Manchester. From the Friargate entrance, there is a pair of small smoke rooms, full of original fittings, either side of a mosaic-floored corridor which extends through to the back of the building. The Orchard Street entrance leads into a truly magnificent public bar, dominated by a semi-circular ceramic counter (probably by Burmantofts or Pilkingtons) in front of which is more mosaic flooring. Originally this area was a separate space but was linked up to the rest by an elliptical arch on the left in about 1995. At the back of the servery are glazed counter screens to the main corridor. Originally there was a 'Market Room' (a meeting room for market days) at the rear but in 1929 this was replaced by the present, welcoming U-shaped seating area plus indoor toilets (accessed via corridors to the left and right).
The upstairs room is largely modernised.

Worsthorne
1–3 Smith Street, BB10 3NQ
07766 230175
www.crookedbilletworsthorne.
co.uk
Not listed
LPA: Burnley
🍺 🍴 (L, E, weekends only)

Crooked Billet ☆

This award-winning pub was built in 1911 by the local Grimshaw Brewery whose wares are proclaimed in some of the window glass panels. The layout is a classic northern one of a lobby wrapping round the servery and with four rooms leading off (cf. the Victoria, Great Harwood, p. 43). The pub is enriched by a fair amount of dado tiling. The impressive servery has retained most of its rising glazed panels. Its surrounding terrazzo floor continues into the front right space which has tiling on the counter front while the other bar counter fronts have fielded panelling.

The screened counter at the Crooked Billet

MORE TO TRY

Here are four pubs in Lancashire which are considered to have historic interiors of some regional importance.

Barley
Barley Lane, BB12 9JX
01282 614808
www.pendle-inn.co.uk
Not listed
LPA: Pendle
  (L, E)

Pendle Inn

This stone-built pub of 1930 underwent various major changes some forty years ago but still has a multi-room layout with a lobby bar and four small rooms leading off, together with various original fittings (although the servery has been moved). On the right at the front and behind there are rooms with 1930s bench seating and other fittings such as bell-pushes. At the front left is a parquet-floored pool room but this has little of historic interest (it once had a small cocktail bar).

Crawshawbooth
591 Burnley Road, BB4 8NE
01706 224267
Not listed
LPA: Rossendale

Black Dog

Just a few original features cling on in this pub, which was built in 1933–4 on the main Rawtenstall to Burnley road and displays windows advertising 'Glen Top Ales' from John Baxter's brewery in Waterfoot. These are the mosaic floor and tiled dado in the lobby, a curved counter in the lobby bar, fixed seating in the room to the front right and a tiled fireplace in the room behind this. Inter-war tiled dados in both the ladies' and gents' toilets.

Lower Heysham
7 Main Street, LA3 2RN
01524 859298
Grade II listed
LPA: Lancaster
  (L, E)

Royal Hotel

A mid-18th century building retaining various features from a 1930s refit including a fine snug, although the historic arangements have been compromised by a refurbishment in 2016–17. Until this the front door led into a panelled passage but this has now been incorporated into the left-hand dining area which itself has had internal walls removed. Adjacent, on the right, a leaded glass screen forms a wall to the snug which has several 1930s features – bar counter, stone fireplace, and panelling to two-thirds height. Everything behind has now been much modernised, although the dining room has a panelled dado in the first part from the 1930s and in the lounge on the right, the bar counter and stone fireplace survive from that time.

Upholland
10 Church Street, WN8 0ND
01695 363236
www.whitelionuppholland.co.uk
Not listed
LPA: West Lancashire
  (L, E)

White Lion

Originally a four-room pub but opened-up by Thwaites with a number of modern fittings such as replacement fireplaces. However, it still retains a delightful intact small parlour at the front (so-named in etched door glass), bell pushes and old fixed seating with baffles either side of the door having an etched design in the glazed upper part. It is served via a hatch with old mirrors either side within the counter but the fireplace seems a replacement. The main bar counter appears old and the bar-back is a mixture of old and new. The rear right-hand room is also served via a hatch/small bar.

Taking it Home with You

Where did you last buy a drink to take home? Chances are it was a supermarket, perhaps a convenience store or possibly a high street drinks shop. It's hardly likely to have been down at your local pub. But up to about fifty years ago it would have been a very different story. Pubs sold drinks of all kinds for customers to enjoy at home and very often there was special provision in the layout of the building to cater for this. Legislation changed in the early 1960s to enable supermarkets to sell alcohol freely and the rest is history. The 'offie' at the pub is now a thing of the past.

The 'off-sales' at pubs went under a bewildering variety of names: off-sales (of course), jug and bottle (and vice versa), outdoor department, family department, retail department, order department, and so on, and you can sometimes still see the old names fossilised in etched glass or doorplates.

The 'Outdoor Dept' (so-named in the door glass) at the Coach & Horses, Weaste, Salford. Service would have been through the sash windows in the screen. The bench allows for the convenience of enjoying a quick one while getting take-home supplies.

'Order Dept.' at the Alexandra, Stockport – an unusual description, but one of many names for the 'offie' (GB)

Occasionally there was a bench in the space in question: typically this would be occupied by women popping down to get beer for their dad or husband and stopping for a quick one with their friends. It was also commonplace to despatch the children down to the offie to collect drink for the family. Where there was no special enclosed small space for off-sales, there might be a hatch facing the front door or one in a corridor. With the demise of off-sales from pubs, so many small rooms or compartments devoted to the purpose have been incorporated into another pub room or turned over to storage. So, when next you see what appears to be a spare door on the outside of a pub, ask yourself this question – was this for off-sales?

The Plough, Gorton, Manchester, has an off-sales hatch to the servery at the end of a short corridor

Greater Manchester

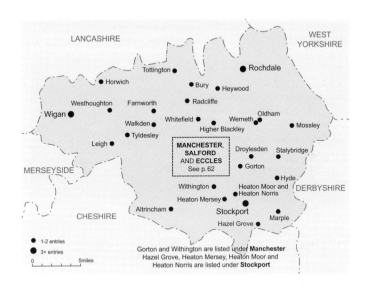

LANCASHIRE
WEST YORKSHIRE

Tottington ●
● Rochdale
● Horwich
● Bury
● Heywood
● Radcliffe
Westhoughton   Farnworth
Wigan ●
Oldham
Whitefield ●   Werneth ●
Walkden ●   ● Mossley
Higher Blackley
● Tyldesley
Leigh ●
MANCHESTER, SALFORD AND ECCLES
See p.62
Droylesden   Stalybridge
● Gorton
MERSEYSIDE
● Hyde
Withington ●   Heaton Moor and Heaton Norris   DERBYSHIRE
Heaton Mersey ●
Altrincham ●   Stockport
CHESHIRE   Marple
Hazel Grove ●

● 1-2 entries
● 3+ entries
0   5miles

Gorton and Withington are listed under **Manchester**
Hazel Grove, Heaton Mersey, Heaton Moor and
Heaton Norris are listed under **Stockport**

Altrincham, Broadheath
153 Manchester Road,
WA14 5NT
0161 941 3383
Grade II listed
LPA: Trafford

Railway ★

A small, appealing but unpretentious Victorian pub which was saved from demolition in 1996 thanks to its listed status but is now marooned beside the parking area of the retail centre that was planned to destroy it. It has a multi-room layout and a recent modest refurbishment has only enhanced its attractiveness. Either side of the entrance are the tap room (left) and bar parlour, named in the cut and etched glass door

The vault

panels, both with fixed seating and bell-pushes. In the heart of the building is a small drinking lobby, dominated by the curvaceous panelled counter and with bench seating along the walls: the bar-back fittings, unfortunately, are modern. Behind all this are two rooms brought into pub use quite recently: the door proclaiming 'Vault' came from another pub. Threats of demolition were averted by listing in 1993 following a pilot study of Greater Manchester pubs by CAMRA for English Heritage.

Bury

6 Bolton Street, BL9 0LQ
0161 764 2641
Not listed
LPA: Bury

Old White Lion ★

Enter this late 19th/early 20th-century pub through a recently restored revolving door and you find yourself in a drinking lobby with the servery (partly original) on the left and a large seating space on the right (the original opening to it seems to have been much widened): the latter has two broad arches spanning the seating areas. But the great attraction is the Oak Room at the rear right. It has wall panelling and a fireplace with 16th/17th-century-style decoration, a decorative plaster ceiling with Tudor roses, animal faces, lions, and birds in relief, plus a cornice of luscious grapes. The party wall to the bar side comprises a screen of painted glass with lion masks and swags. There is fixed seating with bell-pushes above. A rather remarkable feature is the hinged baffle beside the door: why it was so constructed is hard to imagine. The former commercial

The Oak Room

(now pool) room (rear left) has a stained glass window but nothing else of note. The Oak Room is not normally open but access is usually allowed if the pub is not too busy.

Bury

19 The Wylde, BL9 0LA
0161 763 1745
www.thwaitespubs.co.uk
Grade II listed
LPA: Bury

Two Tubs ☆

A building 'of doubtful age' (Historic England) – possibly 17th-century with a good deal of later change and enlargement – this pub retains small rooms at the front with fittings from about 1960. From the front door a passage runs to the rear with old fielded panelling to two-thirds height all along, and further down on the right is a snug. A doorway leads to the small front left-hand bar with a c.1960 lino tiled floor, a bar counter front with barrel staves with brass straps and a copper top. The bar-back fitting has a Tudor-arched central section and display cases with leaded glass windows. Two small rooms on the right appear to have been combined.

The right-hand room

Droylesden

435 Manchester Road, M43 6JE
07827 850246
www.joseph-holt.com
Not listed   LPA: Tameside

Halfway House ☆

A massive Holt's pub of 1912 with a large lobby (but modern fittings). Opened-up on the right is another room/area with original fixed seating and bell-pushes above, and a fine carved wood-surround fireplace. A short passage from the lobby bar area leading to the

smoking shelter has an inter-war tiled dado. The vault on Edge Lane has a former revolving door, original fixed seating, bell-pushes, three 'Half Way House' decorative etched windows but modern servery fittings. At the rear the snooker room still has original seating on a raised platform with bell-pushes above. The passage between the vault and the lobby bar has an open staircase with a fine carved newel post.

The snooker room still has its raised seating for spectators, as at the Lamb in Eccles

Eccles, centre

33 Regent Street, M30 0BP
07827 850252
www.joseph-holt.com
Grade II listed
LPA: Salford

Lamb Hotel ★

A classic Edwardian red brick and terracotta extravaganza rebuilt in 1906 and designed by a Mr Newton of Hartley, Hacking & Co. for Holt's Brewery (cf. the Grapes). It has superbly preserved fittings throughout, including elaborate Jacobean-style mahogany door surrounds and chimneypieces, Art Nouveau wall-tiling and mosaic flooring. From the entrance lobby, with its terrazzo floor and dado of green tiles, a door to the right leads to the vault. This has seen some changes, including incorporation of an off-sales (see the blocked door outside on the right-hand side street) and a replacement bar counter. The bar parlour retains fixed seating with bell-pushes and a wood-surround fireplace. Second on the left, the rear smoke room, entered through a wide arch from the lobby, also has its Edwardian fixed seating plus a Jacobean-style chimneypiece. The billiard room is quite amazing, complete with full-sized snooker table (supplied by

The billiard room. Raised seating as at the Halfway House, Droylesden

Burroughs & Watts of London when the pub opened) and seating on raised platforms for spectators to watch the play. The other star feature is the screened, curved mahogany bar in the lobby with brilliant-cut glazed hatches, still with sliding windows and over-lights. The lobby also has a dado of Art Nouveau glazed tiles which continues up the stairs. Listed in 1994 following a pilot study of Greater Manchester pubs by CAMRA for English Heritage.

Eccles, Patricroft

Green Lane, M30 0SH

0161 789 2019

Grade II listed

LPA: Salford

Queens Arms ('Top House') ★

An early railway pub purpose-built to serve the new Liverpool–Manchester line, although now the internal arrangements are probably late Victorian. Inside the front door is a small, cosy drinking lobby with a hatch-like screen to the serving area in the vault (a name appearing in the window glass). Here the counter seems to be Victorian although the bar-back is a replacement from 1997. Right of the entrance is the snug with draught screens and fixed seating. At the rear of the pub two rooms have been practically turned into one (done in 1996): note the 'billiards' and 'bar parlour' inscribed in the glass.

The snug

Eccles, Patricroft

295 Liverpool Road, M30 0QN

07833 092341

www.joseph-holt.com

Grade II listed

LPA: Salford

Stanley Arms ★

A small, simple street-corner local with etched windows throughout. It was purchased by Joseph Holt's Brewery in 1909 so the work we see today no doubt dates from shortly after this. The drinkers' lobby/corridor is L-shaped, separating the front vault and servery from the rear two rooms. This corridor features green

tilework and glazed counter screens to the servery. The small vault has two old benches and an irregularly shaped counter. Across the passage, a smoke room has original fixed benches and bell-pushes. There's original tiling in the toilets. A former cottage has been incorporated to create a back room out of a former kitchen, hence the impressive cast-iron fireplace.

The tiled corridors.
On the left looking into the snug

Eccles, Peel Green

439 Liverpool Road, M30 7HD

0161 789 6971

www.joseph-holt.com

Grade II listed

LPA: Salford

Grapes ★

Built for Joseph Holt's Brewery by local architects Hartley, Hacking & Co. who were also responsible for the Lamb Hotel (p. 55). This one, from 1903, is the more spacious and has the more extravagant use of mahogany and decorative glass. The drinking passage is arguably as impressive as any in the country with its terrazzo floor, deep-etched glazed door panels and superb glazed screenwork to the servery. The Art Nouveau tiling through-out is very special too: the dado of green tiles continues up the staircase. The bar parlour and rear smoke room also have many original features, though the latter has been extended into former private quarters. A billiard (now pool) room still has its raised seating (as at the Lamb), bell-pushes and a hatch to the servery. In the vault the counter has been truncated, hence the 'stranded' screenwork to the corridor. Listed in 1994 following a pilot study of Greater Manchester pubs by CAMRA for English Heritage.

The mosaic-floored passage in the centre of the Grapes and its dado tiling

Farnworth

1 Glynne Street, BL4 7DN

01204 578282

Grade II listed

LPA: Bolton

Shakespeare ★

Built in 1926 for Bolton brewers Magee Marshall and largely unchanged since. Beyond the main entrance is a spacious drinking lobby, whose rich counter is topped by a carved shield (one of several such adorning the woodwork). The tilework, unfortunately, has been papered over. The lounge to the left has good panelling and a Tudor-style fireplace. At the front right is the 'News Room' (so named on a door-plate), complete with richly decorated counter, fixed seats and the original coat hooks. The back room is described on the door plate as the 'Commercial Room' and has another fine counter. A door at the side of the pub accesses the off-sales, now lost in most pubs but here untouched, albeit unused. The final ground-floor room (rear left) seems to be a private room brought into pub use and now houses a pool table. Much of the panelling is actually modern, now painted in an unfortunate pastel shade.

The lobby bar

Heywood

2–4 Manchester Street, OL10 1DL

Not listed

LPA: Rochdale

Duke of Wellington ☆

The big attraction here is the baronial-style lounge (right), largely intact since its creation in the 1930s. It's entered between two timber and glass screens and has a full set of benches with ends featuring barley-twist columns. The room appears to have completely panelled

walls but actually the top section is a clever design consisting of strips of timber on plaster walls that have been painted brown. What seems to be a plaster frieze with decoration of fruits and leaves is actually a modern plastic affair – just tap it and you realise it is hollow! There is a fine plasterwork ceiling and 1930s timber fireplace with an ornate canopy-style mantelpiece (to, unfortunately, an inappropriate reproduction Victorian-style fireplace). The original stained glass windows remain at the rear.

The impressive lounge has an abundance of rich woodwork

Heywood

Peel Lane, OL10 4PR

01706 369705

Not listed

LPA: Rochdale

Grapes ★

A 1920s estate pub which has kept most of its floor plan and fittings. The entrance has plentiful tiling and mosaic floors, and leads to a drinking lobby with rooms leading off. It has its original bar counter (but new top) and bar-back. The two screens around the doors to the toilets are most unusual. Presumably the idea was to provide a touch

of privacy given the highly prominent location of the toilets (which still have their original tiling). A corresponding screen surrounds a phone booth but this is new work. The vault in the rear left-hand corner has basic bench seating plus the original counter, whilst in the pool room are baffles by the door and more bench seating. Mounted on the counter fronts are horizontal metal bands. Set within the servery is a (mostly stud) wall with a hatch but this seems to be some modern reconfiguration.

The lobby bar. On the left is the small screen round the entrance to the ladies'

Higher Blackley
39 Weardale Road, M9 8WR
07827 850227
www.joseph-holt.com
Not listed
LPA: Manchester

Duke of Wellington ☆

Brick ground floor, 'Brewers' Tudor' upstairs. There is a large drinking lobby with ornate sash-window screening to the servery with swirling designs in the glazing. A lounge in an extension (right) is opened-up to the lobby but has good quality fixed seating. The snug (front left) has old fixed seating with draught screens bearing a frosted starburst feature, and a fireplace featuring two columns and bell-pushes. The vault (right) has more draught screens and a couple of screens to the servery. The short passage between the vault and the lobby bar has one wall with an inter-war tiled dado (but painted over). The brass panel is one of about sixty Second World War memorials in pubs around the country.

Frilly glazed screens atop the counter in the lobby bar

Horwich
121 Church Street, BL6 7BR
Not listed
LPA: Bolton

Bridge ☆

An imposing red brick and terracotta pub of around 1900 and retaining a largely intact plan with a lobby bar and three (originally four) rooms. Many fittings survive too, notably extensive colourful tiling in the dado (partly painted over, sadly) which extends up the stairs. There is much original fixed seating including in a small room on the left of the passage with an arrangement of four semi-circular bays. In addition, there are original fireplaces, cornices and screenwork. Note the dumb waiter with two ropes to move the cage. The large island bar is very recent. The toilets upstairs have 1930s fittings (but tiles painted over). There is an active bowling green at the rear.

Curvaceous ends to seating at the Bridge

Hyde

57 Mottram Road, SK14 2NN

0161 368 5000

www.rossendalebrewery.co.uk

Not listed

LPA: Tameside

  (L, E)

Sportsman ☆

The Sportsman retains many Victorian fittings including tiling in the passage and up the staircase. There has been much opening up but something of the traditional layout is apparent. The servery is right of the corridor and the original counter has a Formica (probably 1950/60s) top. The left-hand rooms have Victorian fireplaces and fixed seating with bell-pushes, but both now have wide openings and the top section of walling between them has been removed. Upstairs is a rare intact former billiard room complete with extensive bench seating and a barrel-vaulted ceiling: the full-size table was removed in 2011. The toilets retain inter-war fittings. Much inter-war etched and frosted glazing exists too.

The servery

Hyde

7 Market Place, SK14 2LX

0161 368 4343

Not listed

LPA: Tameside

White Lion ☆

A rather remarkable pub in the heart of Hyde which retains something of its extraordinary plan and embellishments from a remodelling by Kay's Atlas Brewery in 1906. The impressive entrance to the Market Place has a ceramic surround with a lion's head and pediment (another lion appears on a low level panel to the right). The star feature is the *very* long and narrow left-hand bar and its half-height green tiling tricked out with Art Nouveau details. It was originally probably divided in two – the front part is called 'Bar' in the door glass and the rear 'Vault' (in practice more or less interchangeable names for the least posh bit of a pub). Right of the vault is a corridor with more of the green tiled dado and also the remnants of a screen at the back of the servery. A large section of the wall on the right of the corridor has been removed and the original four small rooms opened up to different degrees. All the rooms/areas retain some fixed seating and there are some bell-pushes.

The long and very narrow vault/bar, White Lion, Hyde (GB)

Leigh

2 Market Place, WN7 1EG

www.boarsheadleigh.co.uk

Grade II listed

LPA: Wigan

A staircase with tiled dado
leads up from the lobby bar

Boars Head ☆

Rebuilt in 1900 with an imposing brick and terracotta exterior (like many contemporary pubs in Birmingham). The interior sadly suffers from opening-out and poor alterations. The main entrance leads into a wide tiled corridor. The most intact rooms are on the right where there is fixed seating with bell-pushes and original fireplaces. Left of the corridor is a bar-hall area with a green tiled dado extending up the fine staircase and down the passage to the rear. The servery counter dates from just 2015, but there is a small original bar-back. The former stables at the rear have been converted into a timber treatment business.

Pubs in central Manchester, Salford and Eccles

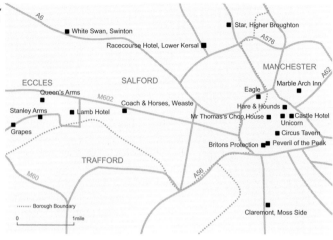

Manchester, centre

50 Great Bridgewater Street,
M1 5LE

0161 236 5895

Grade II listed

LPA: Manchester

Britons Protection ★

The pub opened in 1811 and is said to have been used as a recruiting centre for soldiers to fight Napoleon, hence, it seems, the name. But our real interest here is a major refit about 1930, whence the extensive tiling and quality woodwork in the interior came. The layout is similar to some Merseyside pubs in this guide, the Stork, Birkenhead, and the Lion and Prince Arthur in Liverpool. The

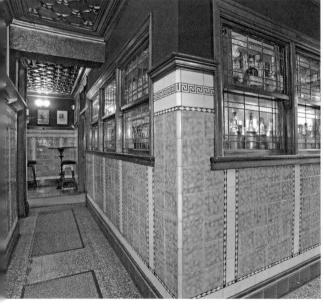

public bar is along the front, and is wrapped around by an L-shaped terrazzo-floored corridor, beyond which are a pair of back rooms (smoke room and snug) served by a double doored hatch with screens at the back of the servery. Especially good features are the moulded ceiling and bar furniture in the public bar and corridor, the 1930s copper fireplace in the smoke room, and the wall-tiling in the passage, which also runs up the staircase. The tiling at the Britons Protection is very similar in style and date to that at the Hare & Hounds (p. 64). The massive urinals and tiled walls in the gents' are worth inspection.

The L-shaped corridor wrapping round the servery has tiled walls and a mosaic floor

Manchester, centre

66 Oldham Street, M4 1LE
0161 237 9485
www.thecastlehotel.info
Grade II listed
LPA: Manchester

The Castle has a rare
ceramic bar counter

Castle Hotel ☆

A small city centre pub with alterations of around 1900. This is one of a number of Kay's Atlas Brewery pubs with ceramic frontages. The interior has a layout of three rooms with a corridor down the right-hand side, where an off-sales has been absorbed into the public bar. A vestibule on the right has been removed, but the mosaic floor declaring 'Castle Hotel' remains and 'The Castle' is named in the inner door etched panel. The small public bar has a wonderful and colourful glazed ceramic bar counter front – one of only thirteen such examples left in the whole of the UK. Also remaining is a fine Victorian bar-back fitting, 1960s fixed seating and a good patterned ceiling. Beyond the public bar servery is a door announcing 'Bar Parlour' in its glasswork and the room retains old fixed seating , bell-pushes and a baffle by the door. At the rear is an extended and modernised room.

Manchester, centre

86 Portland Street, M1 4GX
07863 349957
Grade II listed
LPA: Manchester

Circus Tavern ★

A remarkably tiny pub in the heart of bustling central Manchester. The building, originally a house, is just one bay wide. A corridor on the left leads to two tiny, simply-fitted public rooms, separated by a vertically boarded partition. The miniscule servery, branded as 'the smallest bar in Europe', is under the stairs and is so small that only one person can serve. Its design, with its glazed superstructure, suggests a 1930s origin. Both rooms have old fixed benches: until very recently there were baffles at the entrances to the rooms but unfortunately all but one have been destroyed. The fireplaces are replacements. More than forty customers and the place is packed. Listed in 1994 following a pilot study of Greater Manchester pubs by CAMRA for English Heritage.

The Circus Tavern has a diminutive
servery in its timber-lined corridor

Manchester, centre
46 Shudehill, M4 4AA
0161 832 4737
Grade II listed
LPA: Manchester

Hare & Hounds ★

The Hare & Hounds was given a complete remodelling in 1925 and this remains intact ninety years on. The layout is typical of many in the north of England with a room at the front and back, plus a corridor down one side which expands in the middle to form a drinking lobby in front of the servery: a similar arrangement can be found, for example, at the Swan with Two Necks, Stockport. The pub has both front and back entrances and their vestibules have grey-blue tiling. Inside, the corridor/lobby and front room have mottled brown tiling. All this tiling is very similar to that at the Britons Protection. Both rooms have fixed bench seating but the rear one was evidently the 'better' room since there are bell-pushes for table service: its 1920s fireplace still survives. The servery has an impressive array of glazed screens: the pulleys can be seen in the lobby although the lower panels have gone.

In the front room looking towards the servery

Manchester, centre
73 Rochdale Road, M4 4HY
0161 832 5914
Grade II listed
LPA: Manchester
  (L, E)

Marble Arch Inn ★

This pub, built in 1888 (dated on the side gable) by local architects Darbyshire & Smith, is remarkable in two respects. First is the use of Gothic features in the architecture, which is an unusual choice for a pub, being more associated with churches and educational buildings in the Victorian era. Second, the interior has a stunning display of ceramic work. The long narrow bar has walls lined with glazed bricks in shades of yellow, cream and green. Above is a wonderful frieze flourishing a litany of alcoholic (and cordial) delights. The ceiling features more glazed bricks forming low jack-arches on iron girders, at the ends of which are ceramic brackets. There is also mosaic flooring, mostly in cream and blue with inset flowers, and this slopes markedly downhill from the Rochdale Road end. It is very obvious that the original servery was much longer than the present one. After a tasteless refurbishment in 1954 the arches, walls and mosaic flooring remained covered up until revealed again in 1989 when the present counter, fireplace and seating were also installed. The Marble Brewery was established at the rear of the building in 1997 although brewing now takes place off-site.

Evidently the counter was once much longer

Manchester, centre
52 Cross Street, M2 7AR
0161 832 2245
www.tomschophouse.com
Grade II listed
LPA: Manchester
 (L, E)

Mr Thomas's Chop House ★

This is a fancy Jacobean confection dating from 1901. The front part was originally a shop and offices designed by architects Mills & Murgatroyd and the rear part, facing St Ann's Square was by Woodhouse & Willoughby and of the same date. The interior comprises four spaces, one behind the other, demarcated by light green ceramic arches. A similarly coloured dado runs along much of the walling and the third

compartment from the front also has plain cream tiling, reaching up to the ceiling. The small area at the back has an outstanding ceramic fireplace. Black and white tiled flooring runs throughout the pub. The main changes have been to the bar furniture, which is mostly modern: a photograph in the historic picture gallery in the gents' shows how the servery was formerly located in the third compartment from the front. Over half of this fine interior operates as a good-quality restaurant. The painter L. S. Lowry was a regular here in its less upmarket days.

Looking towards the rear

Manchester, centre
127 Great Bridgewater Street,
M1 5JQ
0161 236 6364
Grade II listed
LPA: Manchester

Peveril of the Peak ★

This pub presents an amazing sight with its late Victorian, green ceramic-faced exterior, sitting incongruously amid so much later high-rise development, but the interior is very special too. A dog-leg corridor serves as a drinking lobby, lined with a dado of green and cream tiles and defined on the west side by a glazed screen forming the

back of the servery. The most impressive room is that facing Great Bridgewater Street. It has baffles by the door, fixed seating, bell-pushes, a Victorian fireplace and a bar counter with fielded panels and pilasters. The stained glass screen over the counter only dates from 1982 but was skilfully crafted to match the panels in the lobby. The rear lounge and smoke room have fixed seating and bell-pushes, the latter also has an elaborate Victorian marble fire surround. The pub was saved from demolition for a road scheme after campaigning by CAMRA and others in the 1980s.

The lobby area

Manchester, centre
26 Church Street, M4 1PN
0161 879 9863   Not listed
LPA: Manchester

Unicorn ☆

The three-storey Unicorn Hotel was built in 1924 of red brick, stone and with some glazed work on the ground floor around the doorways. Much of the original layout and fittings survive with a series of spaces

ranged around an attractive island servery with open screenwork (but there is no evidence this contained glazing in the lower part). There is a snug at the rear and also two more on the right, approached through a triple, timber opening. The woodwork throughout is well-designed and of good-quality, creating a comfortable ambience for a drink. The upstairs panelled dining room is intact.

The snugs

Manchester, Gorton
927 Hyde Road, M18 7FB
0161 223 9671
www.robinsonsbrewery.com
Grade II listed
LPA: Manchester

Vault servery

Plough ★

A basic, but friendly, drinkers' pub of red brick with some terracotta details, whose layout is virtually unaltered since the building was constructed in 1893. The main entrance leads to a black and white floored corridor/drinking lobby with lots of lovely green tiling in the dado. To the right is the vault which is a splendid example of a late Victorian public bar. It has a particularly elaborate bar counter, a fine bar-back in a loosely Jacobean style, and plain, bare bench seating with raked back-rests. The corridor leads on to what is now termed the snug (rear) and lounge (front left) which have historic features such as bell-pushes. The pool room has been stripped of any historic interest.

On the side road is a doorway to the former off-sales compartment and upstairs is a meeting room. Owners Robinsons of Stockport undertook an excellent refurbishment in 2013, two of the many merits of which were the removal of the modern pot-shelf on the counter and the clearing of the off-sales area to reveal its original appearance. Listed in 1994 following a pilot study of Greater Manchester pubs by CAMRA for English Heritage.

Manchester, Gorton, Abbey Hey

187 Abbey Hey Lane, M18 8TN

Not listed

LPA: Manchester

The lobby area

Hare & Hounds ☆

Two small rooms and a lobby bar. The latter on the right retains its old bare wooden flooring, benches, and servery fittings.

There's a small smoke room at the front left (advertised in the door glass) with original fixed seating, a draught screen and bell-pushes all around. The rear room (formerly two separate ones) also has a draught screen, original fixed seating and bell-pushes all around the room but part of the wall at the rear right has been removed. Sadly the attractive inter-war tiled dado in the entrance passage and lobby has been over-painted.

Manchester, Moss Side

Claremont Road, M14 4RR

07900 647657

www.joseph-holt.com

Not listed

LPA: Manchester

Claremont ☆

A large three-storey pub of red brick built by Holt's Brewery in 1929. It lost a revolving door in the 1980s but the curved vestibule remains. The entrance leads into a large lobby bar. On the right the Red Room was opened up to the lobby bar in the 1990s but it retains the original fixed seating all round with bell-pushes in the panel above. The small vault has fixed seating with bell-pushes and a draught screen at one end. On the front left is the Blue Room which also has fixed seating with bell-pushes and a draught screen at one end with a glazed panel in the top.

The front area of the pub

Manchester, Withington

520– 522 Wilmslow Road,
M20 4BT
0161 445 4565
Not listed
LPA: Manchester

Turnpike ★

This is one of very few post-war interiors in this book built or refitted between 1945 and 1970. Work of this period became unfashionable, with the result that it was usually later altered or destroyed. Here it dates mainly from the early 1960s when the pub expanded into the shop next door and gained its part stone frontage. The left-hand bar

The lounge

formed the original pub and the ply-panel bar counter is likely to date from the 1930s. However, the bar-back shelves, quirky fire surround faced with cobblestones, and also the radiators with wood surrounds have a distinct 1960s flavour. The lounge has full-height, characteristically *c.*1960 corrugated wall panelling. Its counter, with its leatherette padded sections, is a 2002 copy of the lost Sixties original – Sam Smiths of Tadcaster, the owning brewery, has a considerable track record for reinstating features removed from their pubs in less enlightened times. The fixed seating is original as is the random-coursed green slate fireplace.

Marple

81 Church Lane, SK6 7AW
0161 427 1529
www.robinsonsbrewery.com
Not listed
LPA: Stockport

Hatters Arms ☆

At the end of a terrace of 1855, this attractive pub, created in 1920, still retains multiple rooms. It was given a refit between the wars and much of this survives. The panelled central entrance corridor expands into a small, well-used drinking lobby where the counter seems to have been fully shuttered originally (but now only the

high-level glazing survives). The most historic of the rooms are the cosy pair at the front with their fixed seating. The small counter in the right-hand one was created in 1999 to replace a hatch. There has been an extension at the rear left to create the long room we see today: its fittings are modern.

The lobby (GB)

Mossley

415 Manchester Road, OL5 9BG
01457 834555
www.robinsonsbrewery.com
Not listed
LPA: Tameside

The servery, complete with cheery customer and dog

Tollemache Arms ☆

Beside the Huddersfield Narrow Canal and at the end of a terrace of 1837, this was converted into a pub between 1847 and 1866, and then taken over by Robinson's in 1926. There is a drinking lobby with an untouched servery at the rear left and then, round the corner, a tap room which has lost a small piece of wall separating it from the lobby bar. It retains its 1920s fixed seating and has a counter to the servery. The small separate smoke room on the right has lost its door and now has a large hole in the top part of the wall to the lobby but it still retains the fixed seating from c.1926 around the room and a stone fireplace from the 1960s. Do visit the gents' – the biggest room in the pub as locals explain!

Oldham, centre

178 Union Street, OL1 1EN
0161 633 2642
Not listed
LPA: Oldham

Royal Oak ★

A three-storey brick pub close to the centre of Oldham, which was given a major refit in about 1930. The key feature here is the servery, a splendid semi-circular structure which projects forward into what is, in effect, a variant of the typical regional drinking lobby arrangement. It is a marvellous piece, provided with still-working counter screens. The back of the servery fits squarely on to the lounge at the front, to which it is linked by a hatch with counter screening. The c.1930 work provided large expanses of two-tone tiling on the walls, a good deal of which has been papered over, unfortunately. The two rooms on the left have been amalgamated into one. On the side street there is an entrance to a rare, complete off-sales compartment which has a hatch to the servery. There is a large upstairs bar, used for functions, with an original servery and mock half-timbering. Attractive stained glass on the landing.

The lobby with its curved glazed-in-servery

Oldham, Werneth

172 Manchester Road, OL9 7BN
Not listed
LPA: Oldham

Royal Oak ☆

This little altered four-room and drinking lobby-cum-hallway pub was built in 1824, was extended in 1888, and the toilet block was added in 1937 when it underwent a refurbishment. The lobby bar has inter-war panelling to three-quarters height. A door on the front right leads to a small room with access to the servery. The small rear right room has fixed seating with bell-pushes above, and Formica-topped tables. The front left room has a lino tiled floor and original fixed seating around the room (but no bell-pushes).

Rear left-hand room

Radcliffe

1 Eton Hill Road, M26 2YG
0161 723 5306
www.joseph-holt.com
Not listed
LPA: Bury

Old Cross ☆

Dating from around 1897, the Old Cross was renovated by Holt's in about 2000 but it still retains a good deal of its original fittings and layout. The lobby bar has a splendid screened servery still complete with lower sections that can be raised and lowered (including a curved one). On the left the tap room and the news room have been combined but retain fixed seating and baffles with inter-war etched panels in the top of them. There are also signs of old bell-pushes around the rooms. On the right the music room is now a pool room but retains original fixed seating with bell-pushes in the wood panel above.

The screened servery

Rochdale

Calf Hey South OL11 2JS
01706 649679
Not listed
LPA: Rochdale

Bridge ☆

A tucked away red-brick pub, probably dating from the 1920s, with five rooms and extensive survival of original fittings including the blue tiled dado in the lobby. The inner twin doors – right with original etched panel, left with replacement panel – lead to the lobby bar which has a black and white tiled floor, inter-war tiled dado and glazed screened servery. The bar-back fitting features some old mirror panels but much of it is new. In the front middle right a doorway leads to a small parquet floored room with what may be original fixed seating. The small rear left room has perhaps original fixed seating (re-upholstered), a new hatch to the side of the servery, new bell-pushes, and has lost its fireplace.

Rochdale

470 Bury Road, OL11 5EU
01706 645635
Grade II listed
LPA: Rochdale

  (L, E)

The plush parlour

Cemetery Hotel ★

Largely unchanged since Edwardian times, the pub takes its name from the cemetery across the road. The entrance porch and drinking lobby are richly tiled with lovely Art Nouveau-style wall panels and friezes in rich shades of green, blue and orange. The front left parlour (no. 2 on the door) is expensively fitted-out with four booth-style seating areas, created by substantial part-glazed mahogany baffles with classical columns. This splendid room also sports a distinctive fireplace with a rich blue ceramic surround and a wooden overmantel: there is also one original etched and cut window. On the front right, a small pool room (no. 1) is rather plain, with fixed seating, a window advertising 'Crown Ales' (from Bury's Crown Brewery), and a full-blown range with the maker's name on it (but surely this room was never a kitchen?). The snug (no. 3) retains fixed seating with a baffle, but its fireplace is a replacement. All three rooms have attractive Art Nouveau-style decorative glass in their upper parts. In the heart of the pub is the drinking lobby. Its counter seems original and the glazed panels above also seem to be old. The bar-back, however, is modern. The unsympathetic wallpaper throughout is an aberration of the last two or three years.

71

Rochdale, Smallbridge
172 Halifax Road, OL16 2NJ
01706 645343
Not listed
LPA: Rochdale

Flower of the Valley ☆

Much survives from a probably Edwardian layout and associated fittings. At the front entrance porch there is a mosaic floor, tiling on the walls both sides and on the left a lovely ceramic panel showing lily of the valley. The core is a lobby bar with a black and white tiled floor and off which three rooms and an open area lead.

Rear left room

The servery has a quarter-circle counter which looks old with modern panels on the front. Above are etched and frosted panels so this may once have been a shuttered bar. The bar-back may be old. The panelled space at the rear right has been opened up. There are two rooms at the front and at the rear left is a delightful small snug.

Rochdale, Spotland
158 Rooley Moor Road, OL12 7DQ
www.thwaitespubs.co.uk
Not listed
LPA: Rochdale

Royds Arms ☆

An impressive pub for its three small rooms, plus lobby bar, and tilework. At the entrance is floor-to-ceiling tiling with a pair of phoenixes, the emblem of the eponymous Heywood brewery. The lobby bar has a modern tiled floor and tiled dado and further tiling on the counter front. The bar-back fitting only dates from the 1980s. The front right room has 'Tap Room' in the inter-war stained glass panel in the door, old, possibly inter-war fixed seating and service via a hatch to the servery. The front left room has modern dado panelling and there is a wide gap between the front left and rear left rooms, and a doorway entrance from the lobby bar.

An impressive tiled lobby forms the heart of the Royds Arms

Salford

18 Collier Street, M3 7DW

0161 819 5002

http://eagleinn.info and

www.joseph-holt.com

Grade II listed

LPA: Salford

Eagle ('Lamp Oil') ☆

Built 1902 in Edwardian Baroque, the Eagle retains much of its original fittings in a three-roomed layout. The inner door, set in a timber screen, has multiple etched glass panels of floral design. The drinking lobby retains a ceramic dado of mainly red tiles and its original panelled bar counter, with screens in the upper section. A doorway leads to the small parlour on the front right with fixed re-upholstered seating. At the rear right is a small room with modern dado panelling and leatherette benches. A door with multiple etched glass panels of floral design leads to the Vault with re-upholstered original fixed seating.

The vault

Salford, Higher Broughton

2 Back Hope Street, M7 2FR

0161 792 4184

www.staronthecliff.co.uk

Not listed

LPA: Salford

Star ☆

A small, three-roomed early Victorian pub that was last refurbished in the 1960s. The tiny bar has an old bench with a heating pipe underneath but the bar fittings date from the 1960s when the counter was moved. The lounge retains original bench seating, which sweeps around the bay windows, and bell-pushes. Old etched glass remains in doors and in a baffle in the lounge. The fittings in the pool room at the rear also date from the 1960s when the room was brought into use. The lobby between the lounge and the pool room has an old black and white tiled floor and inter-war dado tiled walls. The Star was sold at auction by Robinsons in 2009 and is now a cooperatively-owned community pub.

Seating in the lounge

Salford, Lower Kersal
7 Littleton Road, M7 3SE
0161 792 4191
Not listed
LPA: Salford

Racecourse Hotel ☆

Closed at the time of going to press but we expect it will reopen when new tenants take over. This huge pub, built 1930 for Groves & Whitnall, has a little altered plan-form although some of the fittings have been replaced. Both lobbies have inter-war tiled walls and the main entrance has a revolving door. The wood panelled hall runs to the open staircase at the rear and off to the left is a large public bar with one of the largest island bar counters in the country, which, sadly, is a replacement and a large plain skylight above. On the right at the end of a wide wood panelled passage is the vault with old bench seating but new bar fittings. A small completely wood panelled room at the rear left retains original seating. Delightful stained glass details in many windows. Manchester racecourse closed in 1963.

The rear room

Salford, Swinton
186 Worsley Road, M27 5SN
07827 850294
www.joseph-holt.com
Not listed
LPA: Salford

The smoke room

White Swan ☆

A stately red-brick and terracotta pub of 1926 for Holt's Brewery. The most impressive part is the former billiard room (at the rear) with its panelled walls, bell-pushes, curved counter, stained glass, and impressive mahogany fire-surround. The rear lobby has a dado of green inter-war tiles whilst the front one had a door to an off-sales. Two small rooms on the left, each with a good fireplace, have been amalgamated. Attractive door glass also exists with the words 'Vault', 'Bar Parlour,' and 'Gentlemen'.

Salford, Weaste

350 Eccles New Road, M5 5NN
0161 736 1203
Grade II listed
LPA: Salford

Looking from the left-hand room
towards the servery (GB)

Coach & Horses ★

An intact multi-roomed
locals' pub built in 1913
for the Rochdale & Manor
Brewery. The vault occupies
the right-hand corner,
surrounded by a corridor,
off which rooms lead to left
and right. First (on the right-
hand side entrance) comes
the 'Outdoor Department'
which is an interesting and
quite rare survivor, fully
equipped with a bench
and rising shutters to the
servery. Next, the lounge
has original fixed seating
with bell-pushes. A small
smoke room has, like the
other rooms, lovely etching
in the glass door panel but
little else of interest. The
corridor itself has a fine
black and white quarry-
tile floor and a dado of
green tiles. The servery has an imposing timber and glass screen.
Another three sections of this screen are in the public bar along
with old fixed seating with baffles – the fireplace is a replacement.
The pub has been well restored in recent years. Statutorily listed
in January 2012 following a successful application by CAMRA.

Stalybridge

Stalybridge Railway Station
SK15 1RF
0161 303 0007
www.beerhouses.co.uk
Not listed
LPA: Tameside
   (L, E)

Station Buffet ★

Housed in buildings on platform 4 that were part of the station's
reconstruction in 1885, this is one of very few licensed buffets on the
English rail network to survive mostly intact from before the Second
World War (another wonderful example is at Bridlington, East Yorks).
The old core here, the little-altered main Buffet Bar, has its original
hearth at one end, a long, panelled bar counter with a marble top and
ornate back-fitting units between the outside windows. Until 1996,
when the establishment was greatly extended into adjacent sections of
the old station buildings (a scheme which won the national CAMRA/
English Heritage Pub Refurbishment Award in 1998) it consisted only
of the main Buffet Bar plus a conservatory extension. The present
conservatory is a modern replica dating from 2008–9.

The Station Buffet, Stalybridge, contains much railway memorabilia

Stockport, centre

23 Millgate, SK1 2LX
0161 480 2185
www.ardenarms.com
Grade II listed
LPA: Stockport
 (L, E)

Arden Arms ★

This excellent 19th-century town centre pub has a well-preserved interior with simple wooden panelling, bench seating and quarry-tiled floors plus, in the lobby, a floor-to-ceiling curved, screened bar, still with its rising sashes. Three rooms open off this lobby whilst the fourth, known as 'the Select', offers a most unusual arrangement as it can only be accessed by passing through the bar, with permission from the staff. Only two other pubs are known to have rooms like this – the Bridge Inn, Topsham, Devon, and Ye Horns Inn, Goosnargh, Lancashire (*see* p. 43). The fixing of handpumps to the bar-back, rather than the counter, is also unusual. Throughout the pub are three quite extraordinary tables where bell-pushes to attract waiter service sit in the centre of tables rather than, as usual, on the walls. The two front right-hand rooms can be divided off from one another by a sliding screen. Some structural alterations have taken place in recent years, notably the incorporation of the once private rear right-hand room to make a larger pub space, but the integrity of the historic interior remains largely intact.

You have to cross through the servery to reach the Select room behind

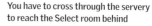

Stockport, centre
154 Heaton Lane, SK4 1AR
0161 480 5850
Not listed
LPA: Stockport
  (L)

Crown ☆

Although slightly opened-up, this pub still retains five distinctive rooms. The vault in the centre has an old bar counter. The front left room off a narrow opening from the passageway has old fixed bench seating all round with bell-pushes. Further along the passage is a slender opening to the

In the snug (MC)

rear left room with more original fixed bench seating, and bell-pushes in the wood panel above. Behind the servery a rather narrow gap leads to a slightly larger rear room with a bare wood floor, more old fixed bench seating, two plain baffles by the doorway and bell-pushes in the wood panel above the seating.

Stockport, centre
12 Little Underbank, SK1 1JT
0161 480 0725
Grade II listed
LPA: Stockport

Queens Head ☆

Like the Circus Tavern in Manchester, this pub is extremely narrow and shows how many small urban pubs must have looked a hundred years ago. The interior was remodelled about 1930 and consists of three rooms and appears to be little altered. The extreme narrowness of the interior led to some rearrangement of some of the internal woodwork in the early 1990s but this was carried out with care by

Samuel Smiths and the pub still retains an authentic historic ambience. On the top of the bar counter (a replacement top) are two sets of spirit cocks which used to dispense drink from the rooms above. The original Queen's Head seems to have occupied a larger building abutting on the east but this was demolished when St Petersgate Bridge was built in 1866–8 and the pub moved into the present premises.

A screened-off snug area

Stockport, centre

36 Princes Street, SK1 1RY
www.robinsonsbrewery.com
Grade II listed
LPA: Stockport

  (L)

Swan with Two Necks ★

A long, narrow pub which has changed little since its rebuilding in 1926, just before it was bought by local brewers Robinsons. The interior is simply organised and the extensive use of wall panelling is typical of inter-war pubs. To the left of the tiled and panelled entrance lobby is the vault, with plentiful panelling, although much of it was actually added as recently as about 2009 (and now covers over a fireplace). The other door from the entrance leads into a drinking lobby, which is essentially an expansion of the corridor and faces the servery. Beyond this is the delightful smoke room which, with its Tudor-style fireplace and oak panelling, has a particularly warm and comfortable atmosphere. From the central lobby one can see the unusual feature of roller shutters which can be brought down to safeguard the contents of the bar-back shelves and, above the servery entrance, a notice saying 'waiters' from the days when waiter service was a regular feature in north-western pubs. A small room at the back came into pub use during the 1960s.

The 1920s smoke room at the rear

The through corridor broadens out in front of the counter to form a drinking lobby

Stockport, Edgeley
195 Northgate Road, SK3 9NJ
07479 942646
www.robinsonsbrewery.com
Grade II listed
LPA: Stockport

Alexandra ★

This fine five-roomed Edwardian pub is very largely intact (even the off-sales, although disused, still exists between the bar-back and an outside door). The spacious lobby has multicoloured Art Nouveau-style dado tiling. The floor is one of mosaic and this was revealed once more in 2014 thanks to the current licensee after years of being concealed beneath a carpet. The servery has a curved mahogany bar with screenwork above but the bar-back fitting has been replaced and a low suspended ceiling inserted. Rooms lead off from each corner, all with their names etched in the door glass – tap room, smoke room, bar parlour and commercial. All the rooms have fixed seating, coloured glass and original fireplaces. Decoration continues up the stairs which are lit by a wonderful window with coloured glass. An attached billiards room has a vestibule entrance and painted glass skylight. Listed in 1994 following a pilot study of Greater Manchester pubs by CAMRA for English Heritage.

The lobby with its curved counter and opulent display of mosaic flooring and wall tiling

Stockport, Edgeley
31 Shaw Heath, SK3 8BD
07931 621220
www.robinsonsbrewery.com
Not listed
LPA: Stockport

Armoury ☆

The interior was remodelled in the 1920s and retains much of its plan form although the off-sales has been incorporated into the lounge (but hatch still *in situ*) on the right. The vault (front left), with an apparently 1920s counter and its name in the glazed front door panel, was once two small rooms (vault and bar), amalgamated in 2003. The front left room has 1920s seating and dado (now painted cream),

The vault, Armoury, Stockport

and an apparently 1920s bar counter (modern top). The corner door was blocked in the 1920s. There is a very small rear left room with 1920s fixed seating. Note the rare rear door glass wording 'Hall', 1920s staircase panelling and also 'Gents' and 'Ladies' door glass. There's evidence too of ownership by the old Bell's (Stockport) Brewery in the interior glasswork. Sensitive refurbishment in the 2000s.

Stockport, Hazel Grove
196 London Road, SK7 4DQ
0161 483 4479
www.robinsonsbrewery.com
Not listed
LPA: Stockport

Grapes ☆

A roadside pub on the busy A6 which retains a remarkably intact and now rare interior from the 1950s or 1960s. Double glazed doors face the entrance and lead you into the spacious lounge area. Here the servery fittings, with ribbed, Formica-topped counter and mirrored bar-back, are really typical of their time. On the right-hand side area is a pair of spaces kitted out with faux half timbering, which contrast strongly and rather oddly with the rest of the pub. To the left of the entrance porch is a door to the public bar where, as one might expect, the counter is a bit plainer than that in the lounge (but the Formica top and mirrored bar-back make a reappearance).

The plain fittings in the public bar are typical of c.1960 (GB)

Stockport, Heaton Mersey

552 Didsbury Road, SK4 3AJ
0161 443 2077
www.joseph-holt.com
Not listed
LPA: Stockport
 (L)

Griffin ☆

Built in 1831, and acquired by Joseph Holt's Brewery in 1921. On the right-hand side is the traditional multi-roomed layout including a lobby bar with a splendid screened servery (lower sashes removed). Off the lobby are a small right-hand room with old fixed seating; a left-hand room with lovely fixed seating and an early 20th-century fireplace; a tiny narrow room on the right (seems to be a conversion

of a passage); another small right-hand rear room with marble fireplace and old fixed seating (opened-up to the lobby); and an area behind the servery with more fixed seating. Holts extended the pub in the 1970s creating an open-plan bar of three areas on the left with a servery copying the old one and re-using the old lower sash screens. There's also a number of 'Griffin Hotel' etched windows.

The servery and its surrounding corridor

Stockport, Heaton Moor

98–100 Heaton Moor Road,
SK4 4NZ
0161 432 5548
Not listed
LPA: Stockport
 (L)

Crown ☆

What counts here is the 1930s remodelling by Clarke's Reddish brewery of an early 19th-century pub. Behind the symmetrical, fairly plain facade, is a layout of four rooms with extensive remains from the inter-war period. At the front right is a small snug, on the left the main bar, and behind each of these is a further room (that on the right is the vault). Within these are the original servery with a centrally placed stillion (a structure for bottles, glasses etc), bell-pushes for table service (in both front rooms), fixed seating, stained glass panels, draught screens and some wall-panelling. The gents' still has the original tiled walls and urinals. Open from 2pm Mon–Thu.

The front left-hand room

Stockport, Heaton Norris
258 Green Lane, SK4 2NA
0161 432 2044
www.hydesbrewery.com
Grade II listed
LPA: Stockport
🍺 🍴 (L, E)

Detail over the vault counter (GB)

The vault

Nursery Inn ★

Built in 1939, this pub lies in a delightful, quiet neighbourhood and is a perfect model of the kind of 'improved' pub that was intended as a place of respectable drinking, catering for the whole family.
It is virtually unchanged, sporting a clean sub-Georgian design and its original multi-room layout. As well as a large lounge (front left), there is a bar lobby area, smoke room (rear centre), vault with a separate side entrance and a plain, upstairs function room, plus an immaculate, very well-used bowling green at the rear. Oak woodwork is used generously throughout and the windows in all three main rooms are charmingly embellished with stained glass featuring all manner of horticultural motifs. Also notable are the rows of what are called 'silk glass' panels over the counters with paintings of drink-related items: for example, glasses of beer, a tankard, a glass and bottle of wine, a water jug and handpumps – all very much in the 1930s style. There are bell-pushes in the lounge and smoke room but not, of course, in the vault. An interesting feature is the folding metal gate (no longer used) in the corridor towards the rear which could be closed when the bars were not open, but which allowed bowlers to use the toilets. The off-sales survived until 2015 when it was converted to a ladies' toilet for users of the vault. The Nursery was statutorily listed in 2011.

Stockport, Heaviley

2 Buxton Road, SK2 6NU

0161 222 4150

www.robinsonsbrewery.com

Not listed

LPA: Stockport

   (L)

Blossoms ☆

A landmark pub originally built in 1824. It was later given a traditional layout of a central lobby and three rooms leading off, its unspoilt interior owing much to the long-serving licensee from 1942 to 1967, Mary Body. A passage leads to the lobby bar (the servery fittings are probably quite modern). On the right is the vault (now pool room) with vintage fixed seating and stained glass windows. On the left is a small room with more stained glass windows and a couple of old settles. The smoke room (rear left) still has vintage seating (with traces of bell-pushes), a hatch to the servery and more stained glazing. Function room upstairs.

Front right-hand room

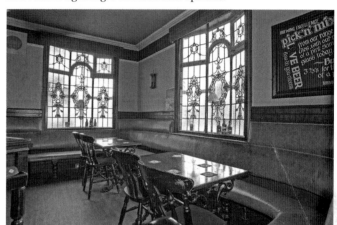

Tottington

9 Turton Road, BL8 4AW

01204 887068

www.thedungeontottington.co.uk

Not listed

LPA: Bury

Dungeon Inn ☆

Rebuilt in 1904 for the Bury Brewery Co. (named in the parapet) and featuring magnificent colourful Victorian glazed tiles by Pilkingtons. The main point of interest is the front right snug where all fittings appear to be intact – benches all round, two draught screens, panelling above with bell-pushes, and an unusual old fireplace.

The spectacular feature is the area above the picture rail, which has wall paintings highlighted by floodlighting. An artist, who was living in Tottington as an evacuee, was commissioned to paint this mural frieze in about 1945. At the rear right is the games room with original bare fixed seating. The main bar on the left has modern fittings apart from some old fixed seating.

In the front right-hand snug

Tottington

43 Market Street, BL8 4AA
07903 300703
Not listed
LPA: Bury

Hark to Towler ☆

An early 20th-century red-brick pub, less architecturally striking than the nearby Dungeon Inn, but retaining much of its ornate interior in the lobby bar and the four rooms leading off it. The star here is the rare ceramic bar counter front believed to be by Pilkingtons and one of only thirteen such counters remaining in the UK: it has a wooden top and is believed to have been relocated within the pub. Behind it are two original bar-back fittings topped by broken pediments. The pub is trading as a music venue and in the rear left corner, formerly the kitchen, there is a stage. The four other rooms retain original fixed seating with bell-pushes, fine tiled and wood surround fireplaces, and two of them have draught screens. Opens 4pm Mon–Fri, 12 Sat–Sun.

A glistening ceramic counter graces the pub

Tyldesley

235–237 Elliott Street, M29 8DG
07584 341099
www.joseph-holt.com
Not listed
LPA: Wigan

Mort Arms ☆

A corner-site pub bought by Holt's Brewery and stylishly rebuilt in 1933. The lobby has a fielded panelling vestibule with a door labelled 'Lounge' on the right and 'Vault' on the left in etched and frosted panels. Originally a middle door led to the off-sales with a screened servery and a left-hand door leading to the vault. The lounge bar retains a screened servery of four bays, all with rising lower panels that are kept in the open position and with decorative etched and frosted panels. The area near to the servery has 1930s fielded panelling all around. The lounge is an amalgamation of three rooms carried out in the 1960s.

The lounge

Walkden

56 Whittle Street, M28 3WY
0161 790 9821
www.brindleyarms.co.uk
Not listed
LPA: Salford

Brindley Arms ☆

A most unusual and remarkably complete late 1950s brick-built pub serving a new housing estate: intact pubs from this era are few and far between. The pub occupies the single-storey ranges, at one end of which is a tower-like structure on open arches and which originally housed an off-sales. The upper part is used for residential

use. The main part of the pub is a lounge on split levels and this is unaltered apart from the loss of a glazed screen that used to sit between the two areas of curved seating. At right-angles to the lounge is the separate public bar, at one end of which is an inglenook-style area with wall benches with an inscription above declaring 'Red Rose Stout' (originally a Groves & Whitnall (Salford) brand). Nobody would claim this as great architecture but it's a fascinating survival.

The fireplace area in the public bar

Westhoughton

2 Market Street, BL5 3AN
07827 850293
www.joseph-holt.com
Grade II listed
LPA: Bolton

White Lion ★

This long, corner-site pub was bought by the Joseph Holt Brewery in 1925, with the fittings no doubt dating from very shortly after that. The servery is the centrepiece, with its still-working etched glass sash screens and counters with tiles by Pilkingtons which, together, form the most impressive features of this pub (the saltire cross tiles appear again at the Golden Ball, York). It is surrounded by a drinking lobby, the vault and the so-called 'Ugly Room' (thanks, it is said, to the

appearance of the former regulars!) where the fireplace has a tiled scene with plough horses. There is also a small bar parlour (the 'John Hyde Suite', commemorating a former customer) plus a refitted and opened up darts room. Bell-pushes for table service survive in three rooms, as does a good selection of etched glass. On the counter there is an old water-heater for making hot toddies.

The public bar with its 1920s curved servery and fireplace

Whitefield

61 Bury Old Road, M45 6TA
0161 798 0088
www.joseph-holt.com
Not listed
LPA: Bury

The restrained, refined fittings here characterise many pubs of the 1930s

Welcome ☆

Built in 1936. The bar parlour on the right has a blocked-up door leading originally to the off-sales that ran down the middle of the present room, which was a bar and a snug until it was all knocked into one in the 1980s. The main bar has fully panelled walls to picture frame height, a bar counter with leaded panels reaching to the ceiling but a new counter top and a bar-back that is a mixture of old and new. The original revolving door has been replaced by exterior and inner doors but panelling around it gives a sense of the 1930s arrangement. The small lounge has fixed seating that may be original.

Wigan

106 Wigan Lane, WN1 2LF
01942 519871
Not listed
LPA: Wigan

Bowling Green Hotel ☆

This large, elegant three-storey pub was built in 1904. The central door leads to an inner lobby with two frosted glass windows. The public bar has its own entrance on the far left with an inner lobby that has a dado of lovely Edwardian floral pattern tiles and a vestibule with frosted panels. The counter appears to be old but on the right has a crude finish and may have been moved. At the rear is a part-glazed partition with more frosted panels. On the right the lounge bar has another vestibule from the central doorway and has a fielded-panelled bar counter. The eponymous bowling green was lost many years ago. The adjoining shop on the right is built in similar style and may have been an off-sales.

The front left-hand room

Wigan
117 Darlington Street East,
WN1 3EF
07827 850210
www.joseph-holt.com
Not listed
LPA: Wigan
🍺 🍴 (L)

Silverwell ☆

A red-brick corner-site pub that retains much of its layout and fittings. It has an L-shaped lobby with some old fixed seating at the rear, a bench at the end, but modern tiled floor. The island servery on the right has old counter fronts and surrounds but a modern pot shelf. Off the lobby are three rooms. Front-left is a smoke room through a wide arch – original fixed seating all around and now disused bell-pushes. On the rear right is a small snug of irregular shape through a wide arch with more original fixed seating. Front right of the servery is a plain separate vault with old dados, original fixed seating and a curved bar counter.

The lobby bar

Wigan
47 Springfield Road, WN6 7BB
01942 201203
Grade II listed
LPA: Wigan
🍺 🍴 (L, E)

The lobby bar and its screened servery

Springfield ★

An opulent red-brick and terracotta pub of 1903 for the Oldfield Brewery of Poolstock, Wigan, by local architects Heaton & Ralph. The main entrance leads to a spacious drinking lobby which has a magnificent counter screen with columns and glazed sashes. There's also decorative dado tiling here. Right of the Rylands Street entrance is a very small public bar with a modern counter superstructure obviously modelled on that in the lobby. Either side of the main entrance is a pair of rooms, that on the right (known as the commercial room) with a little timber vestibule at its entrance, that on the left has been knocked through to an area behind, which opens on to the lobby via a wide, seemingly original arch. Then yet further back is another space opening on to the lobby, now accessed through a crude, modern opening. The spacious billiard (now function) room is a later addition and it's not shown in a possibly 1920s advertisement for the pub displayed in the lobby. Its ceiling and etched glass lettering are quite plain and show how taste became simpler as the 20th century progressed. There was an off-sales on the side street but this has been lost as, sadly, have the once-famous massive bowling greens, sold off in post-war times for a housing estate. The greens had stands that could accommodate up to 2,000 spectators.

'The Bethlehem of Teetotalism' – Temperance in the North West

The North West was a stronghold of the Temperance movement: the 19th-century campaign against the impact of excessive drinking on society and which eventually became an all-out campaign for the prohibition of alcohol.

The concept of Temperance arrived on these shores from the United States in the late 1820s, first in Scotland and Ireland, and then quickly spreading to England. At first, Temperance meant abstaining from spirits – beer was acceptable in moderation – but a meeting of the Preston Temperance Society on 1 September 1832 declared a commitment to 'total abstinence'. These abstainers soon became known as 'teetotallers', a term coined by a member of the

Temperance principles still prevail at the **Cross Keys**, Cautley, Cumbria (AD)

St George slays the Dragon, an obvious piece of Temperance symbolism on Sir Wilfrid Lawson's monument at Aspatria, Cumbria (AD)

Society, Richard Turner, and the message was enthusiastically spread by travelling lecturers backed up by a torrent of journals and pamphlets. Many of these were the work of Joseph Livesey (1794–1884), a Preston cheese-monger who, as spokesman for the movement, became its best-known public figure.

There were few public halls in early 19th-century England, most meetings and social gatherings being held in inns or public houses which, obviously, were not suitable venues for the new proselytising movement. The solution was to build its own. The first Temperance Hall opened at Garstang in Lancashire in 1834, and was just a wooden shed, but over the next sixty years or so hundreds of purpose-built halls were erected across the country. A number of these survive in the North West: a fine example is at Kirkby Stephen, Cumbria. The 'citadels' built by the Salvation Army, an organisation

whose ethos was underpinned by Temperance principles, can also be found across the region.

Inns and public houses were not places for 19th-century Temperance travellers to stay. The first 'temperance hotel' opened in Preston in December 1832, and within a few years most towns and many villages across the country had them. Most had disappeared by World War II, but the Cross Keys at Cautley, near Sedbergh, Cumbria, still operates as a Temperance inn.

Early Temperance campaigners attempted to persuade drinkers to reform themselves, but in the 1850s their target became the drinks industry itself. In 1851 Maine became the first state in the USA to ban the manufacture, sale and consumption of alcohol altogether and inspired campaigners to press for a 'Maine Law' in Britain. Efforts to secure prohibition were led from 1853 by the United Kingdom Alliance,

ANDREW DAVISON

whose chairman from 1879 was a Cumbrian landowner and MP, Sir Wilfrid Lawson (1829–1906), who became the public face of the campaign. After his death, he was commemorated by a statue in Embankment Gardens, London, and a magnificent drinking fountain in his home town of Aspatria. Memorials like this were useful propaganda for Temperance; Preston General Cemetery has a specific area for teetotallers, with their gravestones clustered around the 'Preston Teetotal Monument' of 1859, which soon became a destination for teetotal excursionists.

The 'Coffee Tavern Movement' appeared in the 1860s and attempted to replicate the appeal of the pub without the alcohol, offering instead hot and cold soft drinks, food and entertainment. By 1892 the Liverpool British Workman Public House Company had ninety houses in and around the city, and paid a hefty dividend of 10 per cent on its shares for many

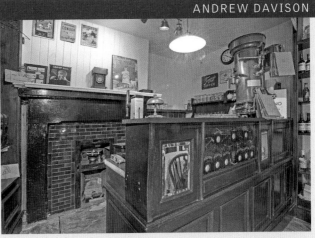

Fitzpatrick's Temperance Bar, Rawtenstall, Lancashire

years afterwards. Continental-style cafés eventually saw off the coffee taverns, though Fitzpatrick's in Rawtenstall, Lancashire, is an extraordinary, surviving example of a Temperance bar selling sarsaparilla and other teetotal concoctions.

In the late 19th century, billiards became a popular pub pastime. Temperance Billiard Halls Ltd, founded in Manchester in 1906 to offer a teetotal alternative,

operated halls around the city and in London. Several survive, designed by the company's architect Norman Evans in a distinctive style with Art Nouveau tiling and glasswork. Most are now in other uses – that in Chorlton-cum-Hardy, Manchester, is now a Wetherspoon's!

The appeal of Temperance declined after the failure of prohibition in the USA. Its tangible heritage can be seen in buildings and monuments scattered across the North West. Its influence on our pubs is less tangible, yet the huge reduction in pub numbers since 1900, the general improvements in comfort, the availability of food and of non-alcoholic drinks are, in no small measure, the result of Temperance campaigning.

TEMPERANCE STREET

Not any more! Several micro-breweries have sprung up around this street in central Manchester (AD)

The coffee house alternative in Manchester (AD)

MORE TO TRY

Here are sixteen pubs throughout Greater Manchester which are considered to have historic interiors of some regional importance.

Ashton-under-Lyne,
Hazlehurst
Mossley Road, OL6 9BX
0161 343 4831
www.robinsonsbrewery.com
Not listed
LPA: Tameside
 (L, E)

Junction Inn

This welcoming end-of-terrace, stone-built Victorian pub was substantially refitted in the inter-war period. Much of this latter work survives. The lobby has a tiled dado and a screen with stained glass panels. It leads into a lobby bar where the servery is to the rear right. The rooms at the front have retained old stained glass work, draught screens and fixed seating. The gents' is intact with a terrazzo floor, dado of green and yellow tiles throughout and four large Shanks' urinals. The passage from the front tap room to the gents' is now used for storage purposes.

Atherton
48 Market Street, M46 0DG
01942 895229
Not listed
LPA: Wigan

Wheatsheaf

A large and impressive late Victorian red-brick pub. The Wheatsheaf name is in mosaic in the front porch. It underwent a major refurbishment in 2017. The rear parts have been opened out but a visit is still worthwhile for the two front rooms. The right-hand one has an intact three-sided screen creating a vestibule-like entrance with colourful stained glass in the door and two side panels. There are also original fixed seats, bell-pushes and a richly treated fireplace. The left-hand room too has stained glass, fixed seating with bell-pushes but modern screens. Note the grand door hinges with large springs. Good moulded ceilings too.

Audenshaw
234 Guide Lane, M34 5BY
0161 336 4635
www.robinsonsbrewery.com
Not listed
LPA: Tameside

Old Pack Horse

This main road pub is notable for its Edwardian cut-glass windows declaring '184 Miles to London', plus depictions of the eponymous packhorse (at least one window is an accurate replacement). The internal arrangements consist of a typical north-western drinking lobby with a servery and several rooms leading off. However, the fittings, for the most part, are of no great age. The middle front room, however, opening up off the main bar has a nice inter-war fireplace with a carved packhorse, fixed seating with bell-pushes and a maker's label 'Sleigh & Jackson Ashton-under-Lyne'. The range in the front right-hand room is said to have been installed some fifty or sixty years ago.

Unique window glass at the Old Pack Horse

Bolton, centre
6–8 Churchgate, BL1 1HL
01204 559060
Grade II listed
LPA: Bolton

Olde Man & Scythe

A black-and-white timber-framed building in the centre of town, reputed to have been rebuilt in 1636 over a supposedly 12th-century cellar, though the present structure owes much of its form to an early 20th-century remodelling. The front right, small room up a step has a bare wood floor, fixed seating throughout, bell-pushes and a shield emblem in the leaded windows. The rear right room, also up a step, has a bare wood floor, old fixed seating around most of the room with bell-pushes in a panel above and a fine pargetted ceiling.

Bolton, centre
127 Crook Street, BL3 6DD
01204 392258
Not listed
LPA: Bolton

Sweet Green Tavern

By about 1950 three properties had been amalgamated to form the present pub, now surrounded by a traffic system. The layout of some six rooms or areas still retains quite a number of 1950s fittings. The opening up may date from the 1950s or could be due to Walker Brewery's subsequent changes. Many of the areas have fixed seating and there are a couple of Victorian cast-iron fireplaces. There are a number of draught screens and some colourful glazed window screens. A recent change has been the careful shortening of the bar counter in 2005. There is wall panelling to two-thirds height in most areas.

Bredbury
Ashton Road, SK6 2DS
0161 430 2589
www.robinsonsbrewery.com
Not listed
LPA: Stockport

Arden Arms

Sited on the A1067, this 1920s pub still retains its original bar counter and bar-back fitting, as well as having lots of contemporary wood panelling on the walls. However, there were changes in 2002 which turned it into virtually an open-plan pub with just one separate room. There is some original fixed seating. Opens at 3pm Mon to Thu.

Cheadle Hulme
90 Ravenoak Road, SK8 7EG
0161 485 1897
www.robinsonsbrewery.com
Not listed
LPA: Stockport

Church Inn

Much extended old cottage pub with three rooms. The main bar on the left was originally two rooms – there is a small snug area on the right. The sloping bar counter dates from inter-war times but the bar top is modern having replaced a copper one. The bar-back fitting is mostly inter-war but half of the lower shelving has been lost to fridges and there is a brick fireplace of similar date. The public bar is a small room on the far right with an inter-war bar counter and fixed seating. Around the room there is panelling on the walls but this was only added in about 1980.

Flixton

Irlam Road, M41 6NA
0161 748 6845
Not listed
LPA: Trafford

Railway Tavern

This three-room (plus off-sales) pub had a more or less intact interior from the 1950s until modernisation was undertaken in 2013 by Samuel Smiths, which led to various modern replacements. There is a lounge on the left which is an amalgamation of two rooms, possibly in the Fifties (which is probably the date of the tiled floor). An arch leads to the snug in the middle of the pub, also with a tiled floor and with a curved counter which seems to be a Fifties survivor. On the right is the off-sales with a black-and-white tiled passage to a serving hatch. On the far right is the vault where the seating may be of the 1950s.

Hale

128-130 Ashley Road, WA14 2UN
0161 941 5367
www.robinsonsbrewery.com
Not listed
LPA: Trafford
 (L)

Railway

A traditional, multi-room pub attractively rebuilt by Robinsons in the 1930s. The left-hand door leads to the lounge/lobby bar with fielded panelling to two-thirds height (counter of the 1970s). On the left are two small rooms. The front one has original bench seating with bell-pushes, and a brick fireplace (perhaps post-war); the rear one has loose benches (the dado panelling appears to be 1960s ply with bell-pushes all around). A passage was cut in the 1970s to link the lounge and vault. The vault (right) has its own entrance but is wholly modernised. The small bar was replaced in the 1970s and is in a slightly changed position. There was an off-sales until the 1970s, accessed from the vault door.

Horwich

175 Lee Lane, BL6 7JD
01204 413449
Not listed
LPA: Bolton

Bowling Green

A three-room, corner-site pub retaining a number of historic fittings and tiling. The vault, popular with locals, is small and narrow and has a green tiled dado; there is more tiling on the wall between the vault and rear right room, and in this area a modest vestibule entrance with a partly visible mosaic floor. The other bar has old seating but is opened up to a small room at the rear which seems to have come into pub use relatively recently. Cut-glass in the doors advertises the 'vault' and the (former) 'outdoor dept'.

Manchester, centre

46-48 Kennedy Street, M2 4BQ
0161 236 4610
Grade II listed
LPA: Manchester
  (L)

City Arms

The layout of this late 18th-century pub derives from a refurbishment around 1900 but some fittings are inter-war whilst designation as a 'Tetley Festival Ale House' in the 1970s introduced further changes such as the bar-back and panelling in the public bar (front). Through the left-hand door is a passage with tiled floor and attractive dado tiling. Halfway down, a hatch still offers service from the back of the servery. Inside are two small rooms on different levels with a widish gap between them. As noted, the public bar with its bare wood floor and fixed seating, has seen post-war changes. Much of the rear saloon décor is from the 1930s: an Art Deco fireplace with bevelled mirror in the mantelpiece, dado panelling, baffles and (probably) the 'ladies' stained glass panel. Another wooden floor here but the fixed seating seems quite recent.

Rochdale
172 Shawclough Road, OL12 6LW
01706 645453
www.robinsonsbrewery.com
Not listed
LPA: Rochdale
  (L, E)

Healey Hotel

A stone-built end-of-terrace pub of 1875 refitted by Robinsons in the late 1930s with high-quality furnishings. The servery has a fine full-height sashed counter screen. There is much inter-war tiling with unusual Art Deco detail. In 2013 the pub expanded into the cottage on the right and a major refurbishment and opening up took place. However, the areas thus created still have many relics from the 1930s in the form of fixed seating, bell-pushes and fireplaces. A new dining room has been added on the front left of the pub.

The servery

Salford, Swinton
135–137 Worsley Road, M27 5SP
0161 793 1568
www.joseph-holt.com
Not listed
LPA: Salford

Park Inn

Perhaps dating from the 1920s, this pub is brick below and Brewers' Tudor above. The vault at the front left has a counter replaced in about 1989, though the fixed seating may be old. The small lobby has a new quarry-tiled floor and modern counter. On the right a large gap in the wall leads to the lounge which was extended rearwards into former living quarters in 1972 and has what may be old fixed seating. There is a lovely tiny snug at the rear with a hatch to the counter, old U-shaped fixed seating and bell-pushes around the room. Some original frosted windows.

Stockport, Great Moor
351 Buxton Road, SK2 7NL
0161 456 6550
www.robinsonsbrewery.com
Not listed
LPA: Stockport

Travellers Call

A small Victorian locals' pub with a plain rendered exterior and colourful tiled dado in the porch. It has been changed somewhat over the years but still retains three small rooms and a lobby bar (where most customers congregate) with an alcove at the front (styled with typical black pub humour as 'God's waiting room'!). The small front right room has Victorian fixed seating and bell-pushes. At the rear right is small plain room, not originally in public use. The counters seem relatively recent. The remarkable collection of bells and nautical brasswork was assembled by landlord Bob Smith who had served in the navy and took over in 1954. Owners Robinsons undertook a modest refurbishment in 2015 including giving many surfaces a modern paint scheme.

Whitefield
71 Bury Old Road, M45 6TB
07827 850218
www.joseph-holt.com
Not listed
LPA: Bury

Coach & Horses

A small locals' pub, renovated in the inter-war period and still retaining its layout from this time with a lobby bar and three small rooms leading off. The lobby bar counter is old but has modern panels added to the front. Note the shelves for lobby/passageway stand-up drinking – at times the lobby is full of customers while some rooms are scarcely occupied at all. On the front right is the tap room/vault with a lino-tiled floor, and inter-war fixed seating.

Wigan
80 Wallgate, WN1 1BA
01942 375817
Grade II listed
LPA: Wigan

Swan & Railway

Now a drinkers' pub, this is a most elegant three-storey building beside the railway bridge by North Western station and which originally doubled as a hotel for travellers when built in 1898. It suffered a serious fire in 1982 so there is much reconstruction and replacement. The original fittings include the entrance lobby with tiled walls right up to the high ceiling and a mosaic floor announcing 'Swan & Railway Hotel'. There is also mosaic flooring to the corridor which is lined with four tall tiled panels on the left-hand side. There are two rooms on the left while the public bar (where the fittings are replacements) is on the right. Despite all the changes, the late Victorian footprint is largely intact. The large high-level glazing between the servery and corridor is from after the 1982 fire.

Tiling in the corridor

Merseyside

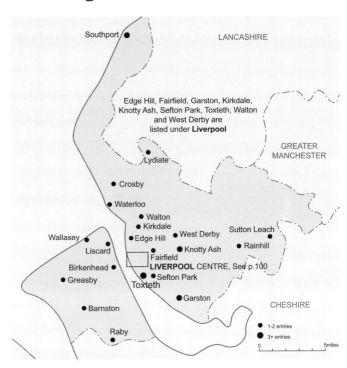

Barnston

107 Barnston Road, CH61 1BW

0151 648 7685

www.the-fox-hounds.co.uk

Not listed

LPA: Wirral

 (L, E)

Fox & Hounds ☆

An attractive pub of 1911 on the footprint of a former alehouse and barn and with surprisingly limited subsequent alterations. The bar and the next-door snug (formerly smoke room) comprised the original pub part of the building. The bar has lots of superb pine woodwork. The panelled counter still has its original top plus a leaded screen at one end and a hatch at the other: the bar-back has shelves with mirrors behind. There is bench seating and attractive window leading, carried through to the snug where bench seating has bell-pushes above (normally turned off to prevent over-enthusiastic usage): bell-box above the snug door. The lounge has two distinct parts – the right-hand end was originally a tea room with bell-pushes, doors

Public bar

and bench seating from 1911. The red-tiled area in front of the servery was converted from the kitchen in 1984 – the range came from a demolished house in West Kirby. The bar-back fitting here, very similar to that in the public bar, was actually only introduced in 1984 and came from a pub in Liverpool and was given additional glass panels.

Birkenhead

128 Conway Street, CH41 6JE

0151 650 2035

Grade II listed

LPA: Wirral

Crown ★

Nowadays this is a basic drinking pub but, architecturally, it is a notable example of a pub with the typical late 19th-century Merseyside plan of a corridor wrapping round a corner-site public bar but with an interesting twist – that twist being a remarkable glazed and gilded inscription running across the left-hand wall of the bar and returning along the length of the bar-back. It's a forthright advertisement for 'D. Higson Wine & Spirit Merchant, Brewer, Cheapside Brewery Liverpool'. Even apart from this, the bar-back itself is an impressive feature, with a broad pediment which includes a (replacement) clock. The side entrance leads to a corridor backing the servery. It has a serving hatch plus a room opening on the right. To the left of the servery is a large room (now used for pool) which has the kind of wide opening that characterises other Merseyside pubs (e.g. Primrose, Liscard and Volunteer Canteen, Waterloo). Note the match strikers on the counter from former, smokier days. The dark red tiling on the ground floor exterior is also noteworthy.

Public bar

Birkenhead

41–43 Price Street, CH41 6JN
0151 647 7506
Grade II listed
LPA: Wirral

 (L)

Stork Hotel ★

A splendid example of lavish refitting, carried out by Threlfalls Brewery of Salford, no doubt in the Edwardian years. The external tilework gives some idea of the superb interior, which is laid out with a public bar on the street corner, enclosed by a corridor with other rooms leading off, as at the Lion Tavern and Prince Arthur, both in Liverpool. The best place to admire the pub is from the cosy semi-circular alcove

where the mosaic-floored corridor sweeps in a curve through 90 degrees. The back of the servery is formed by a screen with a dado covered in blue, yellow and buff tiles with Art Nouveau detailing, above which is a glazed screen with richly decorated glass. The tiling was made by George Swift Ltd of the Swan Tile Works, Liverpool and extends to other parts of the pub too, even down to the loos (the gents' tiling may be inter-war). Leading off the corridor are two other rooms, named as a news room (at the back)

The L-shaped corridor enclosing the public bar on the corner

and bar parlour (left). There are extensive original seating and bell-push arrangements. Note the attractive fireplace where the corridor turns. The public bar has mostly modern fittings although the dado tiling, with a dominant brown colour, rather than blue, is original.

Crosby

63 Victoria Road, L23 7XY
0151 924 6953
Grade II listed
LPA: Sefton

 (L, E)

Crows Nest ☆

An impressive Edwardian remodelling for Higson's Brewery with three distinct rooms where much attractive woodwork and glazing remain. The names of the different rooms appear in the window glass and the layout can readily be discerned, although the off-sales has been incorporated into the snug (front right) and the wall dividing

the two rear spaces has been cut back slightly. The wide opening in front of these rear spaces, with its fringe of glazing, is an original feature and is akin to such openings at other Merseyside pubs, notably the Primrose in Liscard and Volunteer Canteen at Waterloo, both of which also belonged to Higsons. The rear right-hand space operated as a 'Men Only' domain prior to the 1970s when such segregation became illegal.

Private bar

Crosby

119 College Road, L23 3AS
0151 924 5822
Not listed
LPA: Sefton

There is an unusual projection
from the counter in the public bar

Edinburgh ☆

Refitted about 1900 for
Robert Cain's Brewery. An
L-shaped corridor surrounds
the public bar with rooms
leading off on the other side
of the corridor. Dado tiling
survives in the vestibule
entrances and lobby on the
left, but, sadly, in the public
bar it has been panelled over.
The lobby bar-back retains some rising windows. On the left the Blue
Room has fixed bench seating all around. The large rear room was
the result of an extension into a smaller one, perhaps in the 1960s.
Note the inscriptions 'public bar', 'news room' and 'gentlemen' in the
etched and gold painted glazing. Near the corner door is an unusual
piece of bar with a radiator on either side, which has been cut down
in size and this is all that remains of the former off-sales area.

Greasby

Greasby Road, CH49 3NG
0151 677 4509
Not listed
LPA: Wirral

The cosy lobby bar

Coach & Horses ☆

This pub has a compact interior still with four small rooms/distinct
areas which have a mixture of inter-war and post-war fittings. The
front right small room has two old high-backed settles whilst the small
front left room has a floor-to-ceiling 'modesty screen' near a door
which bears an inter-war etched panel declaring 'ladies'. The small
servery at the rear has a lapped wood counter and a bar-back fitting
with a series of drawers. At the rear are three small areas all with
post-war brick fireplaces.

Liscard

1 Withens Lane, CH44 1BB
Not listed
LPA: Wirral

The fine, panelled smoke room is entered through a wide opening from the lobby. This is a feature of several Merseyside pubs.
See plan on p. 13

Primrose ★

The Primrose dates back to at least the 1850s, but was remodelled by architects Prescott & Davies for Liverpool brewers James Mellor & Sons under plans drawn up in 1922. The work was done in 1923 as helpfully suggested by a dated rainwater head. The ground floor has large sandstone blocks but the upper part is largely faced with half-timbering which was so popular for inter-war pub-building. The layout and most of the impressive fittings survive with a public bar on the corner and a servery clasped by an L-shaped drinking lobby. Particularly striking is the panelled smoke room on the left, which opens to the lobby via a broad timber Tudor arch, clearly shown on the 1922 plan and thus not a case of modern opening up. At the rear is a further panelled area, called a lounge in 1922, which, like the lobby and smoke room, is covered by a wonderfully rich plaster ceiling. At the back is a further room but here much of the work seems relatively recent. The plain ceiling here and on the corner of the public bar was installed in a 2014 refurbishment (when the panelling in the back room was painted over). Throughout the pub there is a good deal of attractive stained glass in the windows and screens.

Pubs in central Liverpool

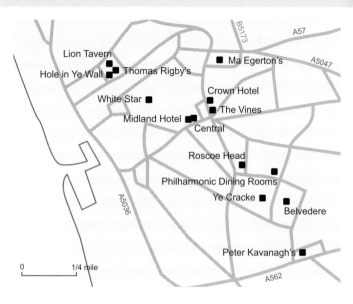

Liverpool, centre

8 Sugnall Street, L7 7EB

0151 709 0303

belvedereliverpool.com

Grade II listed

LPA: Liverpool

The corridor has a counter
and a screen to the servery

Belvedere ☆

This small pub and former hotel has two public rooms separated by
a corridor-cum-drinking lobby. It boasts some excellent etched glass,
notably the curved panel of a Renaissance courtier, labelled 'music' in
a partition alongside the inner door. Particularly notable are the still-
working sashes forming the five-bay screen that reaches to the ceiling
between the drinking lobby and the servery. Sadly, the original bar-
back was removed when the pub was closed between 2003 and 2006,
so what we see today is modern work. On the left is the high-ceilinged
smoke room (so named in the etched glass) which retains an early
20th-century (wood surround) fireplace but the tiles are modern.

Liverpool, centre

31 Ranelagh Street, L1 1JP
0151 709 1218
Not listed
LPA: Liverpool

Central ☆

Built in 1887 (date on the façade – don't be confused by the much earlier date above it!) and right next door to the Midland which also has interesting historic work. Prior to being opened up in the early 1980s this pub had five separate drinking areas but it is still very much worth a visit for one of the finest displays of Victorian glasswork to be found in any pub in the country. The least-altered parts are the two rear areas both of which also have oblong skylights. The walls are lined with glittering mirrors and other screenwork also has fine embossed glass. The glasswork between the different areas was relocated around the walls during the early 1980s remodelling. At the rear is an original partition dividing it into two parts. The right-hand side has a notable Victorian black and white marble fireplace. Also don't miss the fine glazed dome inside the front entrance.

The Central has a superb array of ornamental glass and fine seating (NL)

Liverpool, centre

43 Lime Street, L1 1JQ
0151 707 6027
www.thecrownliverpool.co.uk
Grade II listed
LPA: Liverpool

The rear room with its panelling and richly decorated ceiling

Crown Hotel ★

The Crown was built about 1905 by Warrington brewers Walkers and is their riposte to the sumptuous extravagances of the nearby Philharmonic and the Vines built by Liverpool's Robert Cain brewery. It is a grand architectural introduction to the city for anyone arriving at Lime Street station with the bold Art Nouveau-style lettering catching the eye. There are now two ground-floor rooms. That at the front is a large open area but the various outside doors clearly suggest it would have been subdivided. The finest features are the amazingly ornate plasterwork in the ceilings and cornices. The bar counter has a copper front and there is an interesting bar-back with mannered detail (the mirrors are clearly modern). On the right is a mightily impressive ceramic fireplace. Sadly, this room has lost most of its once-superb decorative window glass (some survives facing the station). The rear room, with the unusual name 'Bar Room' (so named in the door glass) is fitted out with more high-relief plasterwork, good-quality panelling plus a fine fireplace with a copper hood. A winding staircase, under a glazed dome, leads to an upstairs room: it has a modest frieze of crests and attractive stained glass windows, but the servery is new.

Liverpool, centre

4 Hackins Hey, L2 2AW

0151 227 3809

wwww.yeholeinyewall.com

Not listed

LPA: Liverpool (L)

The inter-war fireplace and part of the counter (right) (GB)

Hole in the Wall ☆

This side-street pub retains much from a rather spectacular inter-war refit and has a rare (former) first-floor cellar. Leaded screens form seating areas and while the lower parts of these and the wall panelling are from the inter-war period: the upper parts were restored/replaced in about 1984. The pub boasts working bell-pushes but these are now rarely used (bell-box with three working indicators behind the bar): but if the pub is quiet they will probably be responded to. It claims to

have been the last 'Men Only' public bar in Liverpool, only admitting women when the Sex Discrimination Act came into effect from 1 January 1976. As for the upper cellar, these used to exist in quite a number of pubs: here until quite recently ale was fed down the columns on the bar counter but the pipework has not been replaced so all real ales are now served on handpumps. See the framed note 'Gravity Fed Traditional Ales'. Also note the old telephone booth from the days before mobile phones!

Liverpool, centre

67 Moorfields, L2 2BP

0151 236 1734

Grade II listed

LPA: Liverpool

  (L)

Lion Tavern ★

This richly appointed pub has a layout very similar to others on Merseyside in this guide, namely the Stork Hotel, Birkenhead, and the Prince Arthur, Liverpool. It has an L-shaped corridor wrapping round the public bar on the street corner, and with spaces leading off it. A plan of 1903 shows the public bar as now, but in 1915 the Lion

Public bar (GB)

expanded into the building next door. The corridor was then created along with a news room (so-named in the window glass) in the newly acquired area, and a lounge beneath a skylight (the dividing walls were, sadly, taken down in 1967). The corridor has a mosaic floor and a lovely Art Nouveau tiled dado, above which is a timber and etched glass screen, with openings allowing service to drinkers in the corridor. The back fitting in the public bar seems to be Victorian: the dado tiling here is to the same design as in the corridor. There is a fine set of old carved screens in the front windows carrying advertising, something that is occasionally seen in Scotland but rarely in England. The eponymous Lion was a locomotive built for the Liverpool & Manchester Railway in 1838 and is displayed at the Museum of Liverpool. It was last steamed for an appearance in the 1953 British comedy film *The Titfield Thunderbolt*.

Liverpool, centre
9 Pudsey Street, L1 1JA
0151 345 3525
www.maegertons.com
Not listed
LPA: Liverpool
🍺 🍴 (L, E)

Looking into the side room from the public bar (GB)

Ma Egerton's ☆

Tucked away behind Lime Street Station, this pub retains much from an inter-war refitting in its two rooms and the passage between them from the front door. The passage has a timber and leaded glass partition wall, while the public bar is lined with panelling and retains its inter-war counter (but its top and the bar-back are replacements). The lounge bar has fixed seating all round, side baffles topped with leaded glazed panels and is fitted with bell-pushes. The pub used to be known as the Eagle, run by Mary ('Ma') Egerton, whence its present name came. It was much frequented by artists performing at local theatres.

Liverpool, centre
25 Ranelagh Street, L1 1JP
0151 709 2090
Not listed   LPA: Liverpool

Midland Hotel ☆

Sadly, this fine pub (and former hotel) next to the opulent Central was opened out internally in the 1970s but some fine work still survives. Perhaps the most impressive feature is the window glass which is both embossed and curved – an impressive feat of glass-making. Copper straps across the middle advertise Walker's ales of Warrington. The right-hand strap indicates the buffet for the hotel and this area has a good display of panelling and mirrorwork. This area was originally separated, of course, from the public bar (named as 'vaults' in the door glass). There is some remarkable coloured glazing over two doorways and at the rear of the former buffet.

Window glass (GB)

Liverpool, centre

2–6 Egerton Street, L8 7LY

0151 709 3443

Grade II listed

LPA: Liverpool

Peter Kavanagh's ★

This idiosyncratic interior was fitted out in 1929 by Peter Kavanagh, licensee from 1897 to 1950. The historic core has the common northern layout of front and rear rooms with a drinking lobby/servery in between (cf. the Hare & Hounds, Manchester and Swan with Two Necks, Stockport). Both rooms have fixed seating, above which are large murals commissioned by Kavanagh from Scottish artist Eric Robinson: at the front are scenes from Dickens and at the rear ones from Hogarth. There is also much attractive stained glass made by artist William English, with seafaring themes in the 'Dickens Room' and a miscellaneous selection in the 'Hogarth'. Kavanagh also introduced jokey woodwork, including four panels with scenes set in what seems to be the 16th century, and faces on the bench ends caricaturing Peter K. himself. He was an inventor, for example, of the highly distinctive tables with grilles covering bowls for water to extinguish cigarette ends. The pub was extended in 1964 with a new lounge and again in 1977, taking in 6 Egerton Street. Formerly the Grapes, it was renamed in honour of the remarkable Mr Kavanagh in 1978.

In the front right-hand room

Liverpool, centre

36 Hope Street, L1 9BX

0151 707 2837

nicholsonspubs.co.uk

Grade II* listed

LPA: Liverpool

(L, E)

Philharmonic Dining Rooms ★

This is a truly spectacular pub whose opulence is explained by the fact that when it was built Liverpool was a vastly rich centre of commerce and among the greatest cities of the Empire. This was no working man's back-street boozer, but a place where well-to-do middle class clients could congregate. It is rivalled only by the nearby Vines and Belfast's famous Crown Bar. Built about 1900 for Robert Cain's brewery by local architect Walter Thomas, the exterior is waywardly eclectic, the high point being the glorious metal gates on Hope Street, which are surely the finest such Art Nouveau work in Britain. They lead into what is, in effect, an up-market version of a northern drinking lobby, off which other rooms radiate. The customer is met by

The celebrated gents' toilets are the finest in any UK pub (GB)

the whole gamut of embellishment that makes the 'the Phil' so special – plasterwork, mosaic (even on the counter front), mahogany, copper reliefs (said to be by the German-American artist H. Bloomfield Bare) and stained glass. In the delightful fireplace-alcove the drinker is presided over by stained glass heroes of the Boer War (being fought as the pub went up). Facing the counter are two fine panelled rooms, originally a smoke room (left) and news room (right) with St Cecilia, patroness of music, in stained glass. Further small (now linked) spaces line the angle of the streets. A small office lies within the servery. At the back is a vast room, once a billiard hall (said to have been in use until the 1960s), sumptuously embellished with a huge frieze incorporating the crowning of Apollo (over the entrance) and 'The Murmur of the Sea' (opposite) by artist Charles Allen, also lavish fireplaces, panelling and copper reliefs (again by Bare). Finally, don't miss the gents': easily the best in a British pub (when not in use ladies may, and indeed should, inspect).

The glorious central lobby area

Liverpool, centre

24 Roscoe Street, L1 2SX

0151 709 4365

roscoehead.co.uk

Not listed

LPA: Liverpool

Roscoe Head ☆

This delightful small, side-street pub majors on real ales and cider, and is a huge and revealing contrast to the mighty Philharmonic just up the hill. It has been run by the Joyce/Ross family for over thirty years and consists mostly of an inter-war refit. In typical northern fashion, there are three rooms surrounding the drinking lobby which

forms the lively heart of the pub. Fixed seating remains from the refit, albeit re-upholstered, and there are also bell-pushes in the rear snug. The doors to the three rooms each have attractive inter-war glazed and leaded panels (as do the double doors from the street entrance). In the back room is a moderately ornate plaster ceiling. The pub is named after a great Liverpudlian, William Roscoe (1753–1831), poet, historian and anti-slavery campaigner.

In the front left-hand snug (NL)

Liverpool, centre

23–25 Dale Street, L2 2EZ

0151 236 3269

Grade II listed

LPA: Liverpool

 (L, E)

The Nelson Room (NL)

Thomas Rigby's ☆

Rebuilt in 1852 with a decorative stucco facing added in 1865. Then in 1922 there was a fine makeover which is recorded on the 'must see' fireplace at the rear of the left-hand bar in its rare, dated inscription: 'Rigby's. This historic house was renovated and refurbished by Ashby Tarr Ltd in the year One Thousand and Nine Hundred and Twenty-Two'. To this time must date the impressive heavy timbering of the ground-floor exterior and entrance doors with their lovely ironwork.

Of the three rooms the most impressive is the 'Nelson Room' to the rear, with its oak-panelled walls, brick fireplace, and bell-pushes. Most bar fittings are modern, sadly, from a 2003 refurbishment by Okell's Brewery, Isle of Man. The screenwork near the entrance and some dado panelling in both bars survive from this major refit. Thomas Rigby (1815–86) came to Liverpool in 1830 and prospered as a wine and spirits dealer and pub owner. From his day are the ceiling decoration at the rear of the right-hand bar and cast-iron columns.

Liverpool, centre
81 Lime Street, L1 1JQ
07969 308183
Grade II* listed
LPA: Liverpool

The Vines ('Big House') ★

This is one of the great show pubs in the country. Albert B. Vines opened a pub here in the late 1860s but it was rebuilt in 1907 in flamboyant baroque style by Liverpool brewer, Robert Cain, using local architect Walter Thomas, who had been responsible for the astounding Philharmonic a few years earlier, also for Cain. Inside is a magnificent sequence of rooms with opulent embellishment. On the right is the public bar, less lavish, of course, than the rest and altered in 1989 by the incorporation of a snug and the cutting back of the bar counter (a change which can be readily made out). The decorative ebullience explodes in the lounge to the left with its columns, copper-fronted counter and caryatid-flanked fireplace. The latter is back-to-back with that in the smoke room, which carries Viking ships in relief. Here customers, comfortably seated in the alcoves, are surrounded by wood panelling and deep ornamented friezes populated by busy cherubic figures. They would have been served at the table in here (hence the bell-pushes) and all this is presided over by signs of the Zodiac in the ceiling. Beyond the corridor, which runs behind the servery, is a vast high-ceilinged room (as at 'The Phil'), formerly the billiard room, now called the 'Heritage Suite'. This magnificent room (not always open) has giant Corinthian pilasters, an oval skylight, panelling and an enormous fireplace.

In the left-hand room looking through to the public bar

Liverpool, centre
2–4 Rainford Gardens, L2 6PT
0151 231 6861
www.thewhitestar.co.uk
Not listed
LPA: Liverpool

White Star ☆

Built in the 1880s and
named after the famous
shipping line. There are
two rooms – the front one
containing the servery and
a smaller snug behind.
The old bar counter came
from a pub in St Helens in
about 1988. Two vestibule
entrances have mosaic
floors and old etched glass

View from the back room (NL)

panels: the fixed seating in its own semi-screened-off area appears
Victorian. Note the amazing radiators with figures at the end picked
out in gold. Note too the newel post at the bottom of the stairs with
'White Star' carved on three sides. The White Star line numbered
among its vessels the ill-fated *Titanic*: the line was absorbed by Cunard
in 1934. The back room is famous for being used by Bob Wooler and
Alan Williams to pay all of their groups including the Beatles: the
famous Cavern Club was situated in nearby Matthew Street.

Liverpool, centre
13 Rice Street, L1 9BB
0151 709 4171
www.yecracke.co.uk
Not listed
LPA: Liverpool

Ye Cracke ☆

The historic rooms here are the three on the
right – the small front bar with a plain boarded
counter front and copper top; a snug which
goes under the splendid, ironic name of the War
Office, formed by a timber and glass screen and
with old fixed seating; and what is now the main
bar, which was formerly the lounge, with fittings
from perhaps the late 1960s or early 1970s.
There are two serving hatches in the corridor.
Note the unusual tiling outside on the frontage.

No doubt a unique name
for a pub room

The pub has been extended to the rear and the
far left room has no old fittings.

Liverpool, Edge Hill
2A Smithdown Road, L7 4JG
Not listed
LPA: Liverpool

Boundary ☆

This landmark pub of 1902, which has seen better days, is built of red
brick with stone banding and is clear proof that Cain's Brewery did not
confine itself to building luxurious pubs in the city centre. A spacious
corridor with a mosaic floor and high dado of colourful tiles in shades
of green, light tan and maroon leads round to the stunning high-
ceilinged lounge with a mosaic floor and two alcoves picked out in
green and pink, also with fine woodwork. On the left of the corridor is
a large, long public bar with a high dado of colourful tiling on the walls.

The lounge bar at the Boundary,
Liverpool, Edge Hill

Liverpool, Fairfield
28A Prescot Road, L7 0LQ
Not listed
LPA: Liverpool

Lister Hotel ☆

This local drinkers' pub has a fine polished stone facing and retains some Edwardian fittings and excellent window glass. The public bar has an inter-war bar counter, and fixed seating with bell-pushes. The main bar also has bell-pushes. The fine rear snug has a double width doorway and retains Edwardian panelling to picture frame height with mirror panels, a fireplace with three decorative copper panels in the overmantel, original fixed seating, and a good plasterwork ceiling. The front entrance has an inner door with a deep-etched panel stating 'Outdoor', so evidently the off-sales has been absorbed into the public bar.

Liverpool, Garston
6 James Street, L19 2LS
Not listed
LPA: Liverpool

Swan Hotel ('The Duck') ☆

This corner pub has two rooms and a drinking lobby. The interior is similar in style to the Volunteer Canteen, Waterloo with a central lobby/passage from the front door to rear. It has a splendid bar-back with glazed screenwork to the room behind with service in the lobby via a doorway and hatch in a screen. Opened up slightly off the passage is a lounge with old fixed seating and service bells in a wood panel above. It has a Victorian tiled, cast-iron and wood-surround fireplace. There are lots of etched and frosted panels including external 'Smoke Room' and 'Walkers Warrington Ales' windows.

Looking away from the lobby bar

109

Liverpool, Kensington
189 Kensington, L7 2RF
07548 759106
Not listed
LPA: Liverpool

Kensington ☆

The gloriously outrageous red and turquoise ground-floor tiling sits in front of an interior that still retains a good deal of original, probably Edwardian work. The front entrance leads into a small bar where the counter has a glazed screen which resembles work at the Prince Arthur, Walton (p. 113). Then there is a larger rear room with fixed seating. Here you may avail yourself of table service, a rare thing in pubs these days but the Kensington keeps up the tradition in common with a few other pubs in Merseyside (see p. 119). The public bar on the left is a long, narrow affair but still retains its original counter. The door at the end has three etched panels, the top one advertising, comfortingly, 'Lavatory'.

Kensington public bar

Liverpool, Kirkdale
62 Barlow Street, L4 4NU
Not listed
LPA: Liverpool

Barlow Arms ☆

This pub has a Victorian bar counter with a splendid three-bay bar-back fitting with 'Whisky, Rum, Sherry, Gin, Wines' painted in gold along the top. It has a rare set of 'cash register' handpumps, sadly long disused, with a lead tray and also a small screen featuring a bunch of grapes. A passage leads to the back bar with a modern counter but another old bar-back fitting. This one has two bays with 'Whisky, Rum, Sherry, Gin, Wines' painted in gold along the top.

The servery

Liverpool, Knotty Ash
186 East Prescot Road, L14 5NG
Not listed
LPA: Liverpool

Wheatsheaf ☆

A remarkably intact example of pub-building from around 1930, put up by Joseph Jones whose Knotty Ash ales are promoted in the window glass. The main entrance (with mosaic in the lobby floor) leads to a corridor with a large room with bell-pushes on the left and a public bar on the right. The L-shaped public bar retains an inter-war bar counter, bar-back and dado panelling but the fixed seating is modern. A door at the rear leads to a passage with inter-war dado tiling and floor tiles. There is a wide opening to the rear snug with original 1930s fixed seating and bell-pushes which are still used at quiet times: they operate the bell-box in the servery (with indicators for 'Smoke Rm', 'Smoke Rm 2', 'Parlour 1', 'Parlour 2' and 'Porch').

The elegant second smoke room

Liverpool, Riverside
28–30 Herculaneum Road, L8 4UY
0151 727 4316   www.
herculaneumbridgehotel.co.uk
Not listed   LPA: Liverpool
🛏

Herculaneum Bridge Hotel ☆

Built in 1901–2 by Cain's Brewery, it still retains most of its traditional layout and Edwardian fittings. The long public bar has its original bar counter, albeit slightly damaged where it meets the bar-back. The notable seven-bay bar-back is glazed to allow borrowed light into the corridor behind. In contrast to many other pubs the bottom part of the bar-back has been retained and the inevitable modern fridges are sensitively accommodated under the bar counter. Across the corridor, which has a tiled dado, there is a large room with an early 20th-century fireplace. The right-hand side room and the front part of the back room have a skylight dome (currently not lit). The back part of the rear room, formerly the lounge, is now used as a breakfast room by guests in the thirteen letting bedrooms, and has a fine original very ornate fireplace.

Public bar

111

Liverpool, Sefton Park

66–68 Lark Lane, L17 8UU

0151 726 9119

www.alberthotelliverpool.co.uk

Grade II listed

LPA: Liverpool (L)

Albert ☆

Commissioned in 1873 for Cain's Brewery – see their emblem and motto in mosaic and coloured glass at the entrance. The style is, unusually for a pub, Gothic. Much opened up but, overall, the work is sensitive. The main bar retains its original counter but the elaborate tall island bar-back is a replacement in Victorian style – the panelling, seating and short partitions are also modern. There is an ornate high Victorian ceiling with a good frieze. A full-height timber and glass screen leads to a passageway with an original counter and arch above, an open staircase and a wide opening to the rear right room.

Main bar (NL)

Liverpool, Toxteth

44 Park Road, L8 6SH

Not listed

LPA: Liverpool

One of the snugs

Globe ☆

A well-preserved Edwardian pub. The entrance in Park Street has a small lobby with 'Globe Hotel' in the mosaic floor. The long public bar has an old counter but the bar-back was replaced in 2001. There is a lovely little snug which is surrounded by glazed doors and screenwork. A door with 'News Room' on its decoratively etched panel leads into a small room with a hatch to the back of the servery with a stained glass panel above. The fixed seating all around the room is old, possibly original.

Liverpool, Toxteth
156 Mill Street, L8 6SR
Not listed
LPA: Liverpool

Moseley Arms ☆

A good example of Edwardian pub-building. There are two rooms parallel to one another with the public bar housing the servery which is divided from the second room by an impressive and unusual glazed screen with tulip detail typical of its time. The public bar retains its original panelled counter with match-strikers all the way along, and

a superb glazed, screened, three-bay bar-back fitting with a row of leaded glass panels up to the ceiling. There is a colourful tiled dado running along the exterior wall and either side of the rather fine fireplace: the fixed seating is modern. An inner door leads to the original off-sales with a wood and glass partition but replacement counter. The lounge has a hatch in the screen forming the bar-back, and old fixed seating.

Public bar

Liverpool, Walton
93 Rice Lane, L9 1AD
Grade II listed
LPA: Liverpool

Prince Arthur ★

This is an out-of-town drinkers' pub, probably refurbished at the start of the 20th century. The decorative glass and insignia outside reveal that this was done by Walkers of Warrington and give a hint of the

tremendous exuberance within. Pride of place goes to the public bar, set on the street corner, although the closed outside doors clearly suggest this area was once subdivided. Here bright red tiles line the walls, and stubby screens, unusually, even cover the counter front. The tiling continues round the L-shaped corridor which wraps round the public bar in a typical Merseyside arrangement, as at the Stork Hotel, Birkenhead, and Lion Tavern, Liverpool. This has highly unusual openings to the servery with lovely jewel-like glazing. At the rear is a large smoke room. Gents should not miss the hefty triple urinals, proudly inscribed by Musgraves Invicta Sanitary Ware of Liverpool.

This small drinking area has a hatch to the servery and looks into the public bar

Liverpool, West Derby
86 Mill Lane, L12 7JD
0151 226 9435
Not listed
LPA: Liverpool

The servery in the lounge

Halton Castle ☆

A white-rendered four-roomed pub with two little-altered small rooms at the front. The very small public bar on the right is a stand-up drinker's bar. It has a vestibule entrance and an old bar counter with decorative brackets. The bar-back, possibly of mahogany, has a number of upright oval-shaped carvings, mirrors and a cupboard with glazed door. On the left is a small lounge bar with another old vestibule, a further old bar counter and fixed seating.

Lydiate
Southport Road, L31 4HD
Grade II* Listed
LPA: Sefton

The middle room

Scotch Piper ★

This whitewashed, thatched and cruck-framed wayside pub is claimed as Lancashire's oldest inn (it was historically in that county). Some claim that the building has been in pub use since the 15th century, but dendrochronology has suggested a mid 16th-century date. The northern part, however, is of the 18th century. It was taken over by Burtonwood brewery in 1945, after which the brick fireplaces were installed. A sequence of three rooms, all with exposed beams, runs the length of the building with the public bar on the left. Here a cruck truss is exposed and there is simple bench seating against two of the walls, but the concrete 'half-timbering' over the fireplaces is post-1947. Until 1997 service was simply via a hatch. The middle room has more old bench seating, a pair of hefty wooden posts supporting the upper floor and a massive, much altered setting for the fire. The minimalist far room, with modern decoration and fittings, was originally a storage area/animal shed and later a living room. The toilets are outside.

New Brighton

7 Magazine Brow, CH45 1HP
0151 630 3169
the-magazine-hotel.co.uk
Not listed
LPA: Wirral

  (L)

Looking to the rear of the main bar

Magazine Hotel ☆

Dating from 1759 with a fine double bay-windowed frontage, this is little altered in over forty years. The name comes from the fact that it was once used by sailors who were having their outward bound ships reloaded with munitions. The layout is of a main bar with four small rooms or areas at the front and on the left. The pub is famous for selling a large volume of Draught Bass. At the back the bowling green is still well used.

Raby

Raby Mere Road, CH63 4JH
0151 336 3416
www.wheatsheaf-cowshed.co.uk
Grade II listed
LPA: Wirral

 (L)

Vintage screens create a delightful snug

Wheatsheaf ☆

A timber-framed building with a thatched roof and bearing a datestone from 1611. The main attraction here is the delightful old snug created by settles around a large table situated in front of a substantial brick fireplace. The snug has an entrance gap between an otherwise continuous settle arranged at four different angles. One of the settles has a row of five glazed panels between its top and the ceiling, another has a back of fielded panelling. There are no other fittings of any great age.

Rainhill

12 Station Street, L35 0LP

0151 430 8473

www.johnbarras.com

Not listed

LPA: St Helens

Commercial Hotel ☆

An imposing three-storey pub built in 1890 by Joseph Jones Brewery of Knotty Ash and refurbished from 1927 when the firm was acquired by Higsons. The public bar retains its 1920s interior in the form of its counter, bar-back fitting, dado panelling and fixed seating, but has been re-floored. There is an opened-up lounge bar, formerly three

small rooms – note a 'Smoke Room' etched panel on a lobby door. Here, there are some 1920s fixed seating, bell-pushes, and the counter seems old but the bar-back fitting looks modern. There is a lobby with signs of an off-sales – note the door with an 'Out-Door Dept' etched panel. There are a number of Knotty Ash Ales etched windows remaining and stained glass panels above.

The right-hand bar

Southport

16 Union Street, PR9 0QE

01704 537660

www.guesthouse-southport.
blogspot.co.uk

Grade II listed

LPA: Sefton

The screened servery facing the front right-hand room

Guest House ☆

Built in 1909 this is an early example of 'Brewers' Tudor' but also has attractive Arts & Crafts detailing around the entrance. Off the drinking lobby are three splendidly intact rooms. That on the right has screens (as in the lobby) but sadly the lower panels are lost (apart from one which is permanently closed). The rear room has a wide opening to the lobby under a pretty glazed fringe with coloured glass identical to that elsewhere. The bar-back and floor tiling are modern. The gents' has not just one but two banks of urinals.

Sutton Leach

Mill Lane, WA9 4HN
01744 813994
thewheaty.com
Grade II listed
LPA: St Helens

🍺 🍴 (L, E)

Wheatsheaf ★

Designed in 1936 for brewers Greenall Whitley, this brick- and half-timbered roadhouse retains much of its original multi-room layout. The rooms, ranging from public bar (front left), a buffet (front right) to a small dining room (rear right) are named in etched glass in the doors. The bar fittings, fire surrounds and seating are mostly original. A former verandah (the long, narrow bar at rear centre) overlooks a beautifully maintained bowling green, but has been truncated at one end for the present 'cellar'. The original cellaring was on the first floor, serviced by a hoist in a now-blocked entrance in the frontage. The Wheatsheaf has suffered dramatically from mining subsidence – hence the disconcerting (non-alcohol-induced!) sense of disequilibrium caused by the sloping floors. Much of the interior is obscured by a vast collection of football and rugby shirts and other sundry artefacts.

The buffet bar

Wallasey

225 Wallasey Village, CH45 3LG
0151 638 9345
Not listed
LPA: Wirral

🍺 🍴 (L)

Farmers Arms ☆

Rebuilt in 1924 and still retaining three rooms, with much panelling, a part-glazed partition wall and leaded glass from that date. On the right is a small L-shaped public bar with bare bench seating and bell-pushes; the bar-back

Partitions seen from the public bar

appears to date from the 1920s, but the counter is a replacement. However, the counter on the left-hand lobby side with a curved top section would appear to date from the rebuild.

Waterloo

45 East Street, L22 8QR

07891 407464

Grade II listed

LPA: Sefton

Volunteer Canteen ★

The pub was established here in 1871 and its interior was remodelled in 1924 by Higsons of Toxteth, whose name lives on in the window glass. There have been few major changes since. A central doorway leads into a panelled corridor, on the right of which is an opening into the servery. On either side are service hatches with glazed panels above. On the left side of the corridor is a broad archway which seems original to 1924 and opens into the lounge. The bell-pushes were regrettably removed quite recently but this is still a rare example of a pub where customers can be served at their tables (except at busy times, of course). The cupboards and rather crude mirrorwork on the rear wall are modern work, although the fire surround and seating are evidently of the 1920s. On the right-hand side is a public bar with 1924 bar-back and counter; the latter has a new top and modern pot-shelf. The toilets retain their 1924 doors, each labelled with the appropriate gender in the glazing.

The servery seen through a wide arch from the right-hand room (GB)

Table Service – a Merseyside Survival

In many an old pub you will find bell-pushes dotted round a room. Only at a handful do they still work, but they are a reminder of a largely forgotten practice – table service. The bells were connected to a box in the servery where a bell would ring and an indicator would wobble to show where a customer was requiring a drink. A member of the servery staff or a dedicated waiter would then go and take the order. Needless to say prices were a touch higher than in the public bar and a copper or two by way of a tip for the waiter was usual.

The editor of this guide began his under-age drinking in Birmingham in the early 1960s and was blissfully unaware of this concept. Moving to Manchester he was surprised by this wholly new experience of guys (and I think it was always men) coming round to take orders. It worked very efficiently as the waiting staff went to a dedicated area of the counter from which other customers were

Annunciator box at the Springfield, Wigan, Greater Manchester (Mark Finney)

excluded so they did not have to fight their way through a crowd of stand-up drinkers.

Has this very civilised way of carrying on now vanished? Not quite. It still takes place on Merseyside where it is still alive and well at a few pubs provided things aren't too busy. Two of the most famous examples are Crows Nest, Crosby (p. 97), and Volunteer Canteen, Waterloo (p. 118). It's also to be found occasionally at the Hole in Ye Wall, and is expected to be re-introduced at the Kensington, both in Liverpool. A wonderful tradition continued.

Bell-push at the Vines, Liverpool (GB)

At the Arden Arms, Stockport, bell-pushes are to be found in the middle of several tables

Table service is still alive and well at the Volunteer Canteen, Waterloo, Merseyside (GB)

MORE TO TRY

Here are eight pubs in Merseyside which are considered to have historic interiors of some regional importance.

Earlestown
2 Earle Street, WA12 9LN
Not listed
LPA: St Helens

Rams Head

A once-impressive Edwardian town centre pub is worth a visit because, whilst having undergone a number of changes over the years, it retains several features of interest both from the first build and a subsequent inter-war refit. These include the servery which has two 'shop window' style hatches with two rows of windows above the hatches, a tiled dado (including all the way up the stairs), and fixed seating. Lovely mosaic-work in the entrance lobby.

Huyton
39 Blacklow Brow, L36 5XE
Not listed
LPA: Knowsley

Queens Arms (GB)

Queens Arms

A framed letter dated 21 May 1957 from David J. Lewis, architect of Angel Buildings, 20 Dale Street, Liverpool to Peter Walker's Brewery of Warrington, quotes a builder's estimate of £25,153 to re-build the Queens Arms. Above a picture shows the Victorian predecessor. The new pub, built of brick with a rendered upper floor, was very conservative in style, reminiscent of the 1930s. The two bars are rather austere affairs but they do retain a large amount of original fittings, notably the bar-backs and counters. The detailing of the woodwork is very chunky in the supports to the superstructure over the counter in the left-hand bar and the bold ribbing on the right-hand counter. Note the rather delightful sliding door to the rear of the left-hand part of the servery. Some modern change has also taken place, chiefly noticeable in the dado panelling and the loss of an off-sales facing the front entrance. There is a blocked corner doorway on the left-hand side which might suggest a former internal subdivision. What is for sure is that there was an off-sales facing the front entrance.

Liverpool, centre
133 Dale Street, L2 2JH
0151 236 0859
www.theshipandmitre.com
Not listed
LPA: Liverpool
  ⅋(L, E)

Ship & Mitre

Built in 1936–7 with brick and fine white stone facing, this pub was the Bents Brewery Tap and overlooks the entrance to Birkenhead Tunnel, opened in 1933. The downstairs bar was modernised in 1985 but the panelled upper room remains largely as built. It operates as a function room but may be viewed by asking the staff. Do visit the gents' with its illuminated 1930s sign to see its terrazzo floor, hand-painted tiles depicting sportsmen, and three big urinals by Dodd & Oulton Ltd, Liverpool.

Liverpool, Garston
79 St Mary's Road, L19 2NL
Not listed
LPA: Liverpool

Dealers Arms

Rebuilt in about 1930 with elegant off-white faience facing, this pub has two main bars. That on the right has its original vestibule entrance. It has been opened up to a small rear room which has inter-war fixed seating with panelling above. A side doorway, with glass labelled 'smoke room', leads to the left-hand spaces and the front bar retains the original counter, fixed seating and panelling above. The rear room has original fixed seating and fielded panelling above seating to two-thirds height. Sadly, the character of the interior has been much altered by the liberal use of pastel paint (the original finish does survive in some places so you can spot the contrast). The name of the pub, etched in several windows and its meaning, is spelled out on the pub sign where two men down at the docks look set to do some dodgy business.

Liverpool, Kirkdale
86 Fountains Road, L4 1ST
0151 922 2147
Not listed
LPA: Liverpool

Saddle

A corner pub with a blocky, red-brick faced exterior and a fine Threlfall's window in the doorway. Inside a passage leads to the lobby bar. Carefully renovated in recent years, it retains a number of old features especially the extensive tiled dado in the lobby bar and passageway and also up the staircase and to the toilets. Also noteworthy are the fixed seating and bell-pushes, as in the opened-up room on the right.

Liverpool, Toxteth
131 Parkhill Road, L8 4RN
Not listed
LPA: Liverpool

Bleak House

The upper section of the bar-back fitting is old with advertising for brewers D. Higson at the top: the lower section is modern. The bar counter has been moved and originally went as far as the cast-iron pillar. On the left up three steps is a snug area which was a separate room until 1994 and has a cast-iron fireplace and old seating. The parlour retains inter-war fixed seating, a Victorian fireplace and has a hatch to the back of the bar.

Liverpool, West Derby
2 Leyfield Road, L12 9HA
Not listed
LPA: Liverpool

Crown

Rebuilt in 1935 to designs by Liverpool architects Medcalf & Medcalf (their perspective drawing hangs in the left-hand bar) and retaining a number of features from that time. Following the comprehensive remodelling of the large left-hand bar in the 1970s, these are best appreciated in the L-shaped public bar with fielded panelling all round, and the snug (usually shut but can be opened on request), also panelled, with bell-pushes above the bare bench seating. Note the 'Crown Inn Bowling Club' honours board – the club still plays on the green at the back. The central door at the front led to a former off-sales.

Liverpool, Woolton
2 Acrefield Road, L25 5JL
0151 428 2255
Not listed
LPA: Liverpool
 (L)

White Horse

This pub has a very appealing inter-war interior and, despite much opening up, the essentials of the layout then created can be appreciated. The counter and four-bay bar-back are largely original (despite such inevitable changes such as the fridges and new shelves) and there are also contemporary dado panelling, fixed seating and baffles. The small front right room is perhaps the most intact space with its fixed seating, baffles and bell-pushes but the wall panelling is modern as is much of the work in the opened-up rear right space. There are a series of ornamented ceiling panels in all areas of the pub. The front windows have etched glass, those on the right being notable for being curved.

Pub listings   # Isle of Man

Douglas
3 Chapel Row, IM1 2BJ
01624 673632
Not registered
LPA: Isle of Man

Albert Hotel ☆

This pub, next to the bus station, was first licensed in 1862 and has had various names over the years. It has also had refits, the latest being back in the 1960s. The right-hand public bar has ply panelling painted a mahogany colour and two sections of fixed bench seating with red-button leatherette covering. The left-hand saloon also has ply panelling painted mahogany and a section of fixed bench seating taking up three sides of the rear. The servery opens to both bars and has ply-panel counter fronts and modest wood shelves. A typical modest (and cheap) refit of the 1960s.

Public bar (PK)

Peel
2 Tynwald Road, IM5 1LA
01624 842252
Not registered
LPA: Isle of Man

White House ☆

Built in the 19th century and substantially remodelled in Edwardian times and again in the 1930s, when a large extension was added to the left and rear, and refurbished yet again in the late 1960s. A lobby bar has glazed sashes (no longer working). The small front bar has a venerable baffle and some fixed seating but the bar counter is modern. The rear room and right-hand room were refurbished in the late 1960s and have some decent wood-panelled bench seating and an Edwardian fireplace, but the rest is typical of the late 1960s and of no real merit. One of the few pubs on the island to sell real cider.

The servery and its screened counter (PK)

The Selection Criteria for CAMRA's Inventories

What really matters about a pub is its interior. CAMRA's inventories of historic pub interiors focus entirely on the **internal physical fabric** of pubs and what is **authentically old** inside them. In this context a pub's external architecture, fine though it may be, is a side issue.

National or regional significance?
The pubs that qualify for the National Inventory of Historic Pub Interiors (NI) must have outstanding attributes – either a high degree of internal intactness or, where there has been alteration, some truly exceptional features or rooms. Outstanding bars and pub-type rooms in other kinds of licensed establishment, such as hotel bars, theatre bars or railway buffets, are also embraced. Rather less is expected of candidates for a Regional Inventory of historic pub interiors (RI), although they must retain a significant amount of genuine historic features and/or a good sense of their historic layout.

Age
The main focus is on interiors from before the Second World War, i.e. 1939, but some later ones that have survived unaltered, especially from before the mid-1960s (when the modern mania for pub refitting and opening-out began in earnest) are now rare and have to be seriously considered too. There is, however, a need for more research to develop appropriate criteria for post-war pubs, and at the time of writing, CAMRA is assisting Historic England with an in-depth study of this largely unrecognised era for pubs. In the meantime, CAMRA is careful to restrict its present selections to clear cases that have special merit. Interiors after 1970 do not qualify at all.

Historic pub fittings, features and plan-form
The emphasis is on items that reflect the premises' historic function **as a pub**, rather than inherited from some other (usually domestic) use of the building, although the line is not always easy to draw. Items of specific interest include such things as servery fittings, fixed settles or bench seating, screens, bell-pushes, and original toilets as well as fittings and décor purpose-designed for pubs. If such features as these survive in abundance, with little lost, the pub is a clear candidate for the NI.

The survival of historic layout is also a crucial factor in assessing NI candidates, but Regional Inventory candidates too should retain sufficient for their original planning to be appreciated and understood. Where a pub has undergone modern extension, this need not count against it providing the work has been sensitively done and does not seriously compromise its historic core.

The bottom line?
If all that's left is a couple of fixed benches and a bit of matchboard panelling in a largely opened-up pub, inclusion will not be justified as such things are commonplace. Many interiors too still have a few old features like etched glass or tilework which are irreplaceable and a joy to behold but CAMRA has been cautious about developing plans for a nationally-led campaign to identify and catalogue them – the hope being that the inspiration for compiling 'local inventories' will take off at the local level itself. Work done by Sheffield & District Branch of CAMRA in identifying and describing such pubs in their area shows what a worthwhile exercise this can be.

Factual evidence and informed judgement
CAMRA's inventories set great store by including only what is *genuinely* old. This ought to be a matter of objective, provable fact and certainly the selections for the North West Regional Inventory have been authenticated wherever possible from documentary sources like original plans, building records or other archive material. However, where no such material exists, as is all too often the case, the truth is not always easy to establish. Oral testimony from licensees and older regulars can be an invaluable help but reliance often has to be placed on experience and informed judgement.

Glossary

Ale: originally a fermented malt liquor, made without the use of hops. The term has been effectively interchangeable with 'beer' for at least 200 years.

Art Deco: a fashionable style between the two world wars in Europe and America. It relied on geometrical patterns and sleek lines. The name comes from the Exposition Internationale des Arts Décoratifs et Industriels Modernes held in Paris in 1925 which greatly enhanced its popularity, although the diverse styles that characterize Art Deco had already appeared in Paris and Brussels before World War I.

Art Nouveau: a style relying on flowing lines and sinuous forms, and often based on nature and the human figure. It was popular from about 1890 until 1914, but more in Europe than the UK.

Bar-back: the shelving etc. at the rear of the servery, sometimes very ornately treated, for example, with mirrors. In Scotland and Northern Ireland known as a gantry.

Barrel: although widely used as a term for any size of cask, the term applies, strictly speaking, to a vessel containing 36 gallons. It used to be the standard size for beer casks until the mid-20th century. Nowadays the standard cask contains nine gallons and is properly termed a firkin.

Bottle and jug: *see* off-sales.

Brewers' Tudor: a style, especially popular between the two world wars, drawing nostalgically upon the half-timbered architecture of the Tudor period. Within pubs it was often associated with fully panelled rooms.

Brewery tap: a brewery's nearest tied retail outlet.

'Carlisle Experiment': *see* next entry.

Carlisle State Management Scheme: the scheme under which brewing and pubs in the Carlisle area were taken into State control during the First World War and lasting until the 1970s (*see* pp. 34–5).

Commercial room: a popular, traditional pub room name in the North West for a space that would have been rather more tranquil than the public bar and where, in all probability, commercial travellers and traders might do business. It would have had a similar character to a newsroom.

Counter screens: glazed screens mounted on counters and popular in the North West. Many had/have sash windows that could be raised and lowered (*see* Index for the best examples illustrated in this guide).

Dado: the lower part of a wall, often but not always below a rail and above a skirting board.

Drinking lobby/corridor: an area for almost exclusively stand-up drinking, and popular in the north of England. Often the lobby is in the heart of the pub with rooms radiating off it (*see* Index for illustrations of good examples in this guide). Occasionally it lies on a corridor with a widened area in front of the servery.

Fielded panelling: square panels with recessed centres.

Formica: a laminate product, very popular in the 1950s and 1960s, for counter tops or other surfaces needing to be kept clean.

Improved public houses: inter-war ones built with the aim of making the pub respectable. They tended to be large, had a wide range of facilities, and sought to attract a better class of customer.

Inglenook: a recess, often very substantial, adjoining a fireplace.

Inn: premises offering drink, food and accommodation for travellers in earlier centuries. More recently the term has been loosely used by any kind of pub establishment (likewise tavern, q.v.).

Jug and bottle: *see* off-sales.

Leatherette: an artificial leather product, made by covering a fabric base with plastic.

Lounge: a better-class pub room.

Moderne: a fairly modest, sleek and rather simplified version of Art Deco (q.v.). It featured curving forms and smooth, polished surfaces.

News room: a traditional pub room name in the North West, for a space probably similar in character to a commercial room (q.v.).

Off-sales: sale of drinks for consumption off the premises. Off-sales compartments went under a variety of names: the jug and bottle, bottle and jug, outdoor department, family department etc.

Outdoor department: *see* off-sales.

Pediment: a triangular or sometimes curved gable.

Pubco: a pub-owning company with no brewing interests.

Public house: Literally a house open to the public. The name refers back to much earlier centuries when individuals would open their houses for the sale of drink. In the 19th century 'public house' tended to refer to fully licensed premises selling all types of intoxicating liquor, as opposed to beerhouses which sold just beer.

Quarry tiles: plain, unglazed floor tiles, usually red and black.

Real ale: a term coined in the early 1970s to describe traditional British beer, which undergoes a secondary fermentation and conditioning in the cask (hence the alternative term 'cask-conditioned').

Roadhouse: a (usually large) inter-war pub beside a main road, often with extensive facilities to attract, for example, families and the new generation of motorists. See also improved public houses.

Screened servery: *see* counter screens.

Servery: the area from which drinks are dispensed.

Settle: bench seating, often curved, with a medium to high back.

Smoke room: a better-class pub room.

Snug: a small, intimate drinking space.

Spittoon trough: a shallow trough, most commonly met with in public bars, about eight inches wide, usually made of terrazzo (q.v.) and which formed a receptacle for sundry detritus, slops and, quite literally, spit. Both spit and sawdust were commonplace in the public bar and have given rise to a phrase to describe a fairly basic building or room.

Tap room: a pub room of similar status to the public bar. Despite what the name might suggest, drink was very rarely dispensed within them as they tended to be separate from the servery.

Tavern: originally an urban drinking house serving wine and food, mostly to better-off customers. In modern times the term has been adopted by all kinds of pub establishment (likewise inn, q.v.).

Teetotal: abstaining from all alcoholic drinks.

Temperance: advocacy of drinking little or no alcohol (*see also* pp. 88–9). The earliest campaigners about 1830 promoted moderation and boycotted only spirits: however, after 1832 increasing numbers became teetotal (q.v.).

Terracotta: (literally fired earth): hard-wearing, unglazed ceramic ware.

Terrazzo: tiny pieces of marble set in concrete, rubbed down and polished.

Vault: an alternative name for a public bar in the North West of England.

Editor's Acknowledgements

Firstly, Pub Heritage Group (PHG) wishes to record its enormous gratitude to Liverpool & Districts CAMRA for generous financial support in the preparation of this guide and which has made it possible.

During the eighteen months this guide has been under preparation, many individuals have helped in many ways to make the guide a reality. Members of PHG have been unstinting in their support, and special thanks for work on the texts go to (alphabetically), Paul Ainsworth, chair of the Group for his general support for the project and writing much of the introductory material; Andrew Davison for his informative articles about the influential Temperance Movement and the 'Carlisle Experiment'; Michael Croxford for editing so many of our long, website descriptions into concise ones and also for invaluable proof-reading; Steve Peck, also for heroic proof-reading work; and Chris Witt for managing the project in terms of administration and budgeting for PHG.

Guides such as this depend heavily on having good illustrations and the majority here have been generously provided by Michael Slaughter from his astonishing collection which effectively amounts to the nation's photo archive of historic pub interiors. Michael Croxford, Andrew Davison, Neil Lloyd and others have also kindly supplied photographs which are indicated by their initials. The maps that are so important in helping people understand the geography of the pubs have been expertly produced by Alan and Julie Snook.

Many people have supplied information about particular pubs but special thanks must go to Emily Cole of Historic England whose colleagues have unearthed much valuable information during their survey work on inter-war and post-war pubs and which is incorporated here.

PHG would like to extend its thanks to Simon Hall and Julie Hudson at CAMRA Books for their professional advice and help in the preparation of this guide, and also to the designer, Dale Tomlinson, whose excellent, appealing work will, hopefully, entice you to visit many of these precious and interesting pubs.

Index

Pub entries appearing in the gazetteer are not indexed here: other references to them (under place name) are listed here with their county (Ch – Cheshire, Cu – Cumbria, La – Lancashire, GM – Greater Manchester, Me – Merseyside).

Page numbers in *italics* refer to illustrations

Books for pub & beer lovers

CAMRA Books, the publishing arm of the Campaign for Real Ale, is the leading publisher of books on beer and pubs. Key titles include:

Good Beer Guide 2018

Edited by **ROGER PROTZ**

CAMRA's *Good Beer Guide* is fully revised and updated each year and features pubs across the United Kingdom that serve the best real ale. Now in its 45th edition, this pub guide is completely independent with listings based entirely on nomination and evaluation by CAMRA members. This means you can be sure that every one of the 4,500 pubs deserves their place, plus they all come recommended by people who know a thing or two about good beer.

£15.99   ISBN 978 1 85249 344 8   *Available September 2017*

Britain's Best Real Heritage Pubs *New Edition*
GEOFF BRANDWOOD

This definitive listing is the result of 25 years' research by CAMRA to discover pubs that are either unaltered in 70 years or have features of truly national historic importance. Fully revised from the 2013 edition, the book boasts updated information and a new set of evocative illustrations. Among the 260 pubs, there a re unspoilt country locals, Victorian drinking palaces and mighty roadhouses. The book has features describing how the pub developed and what's distinctive about pubs in different parts of the country.

£9.99   ISBN 978 1 85249 334 9

Yorkshire's Real Heritage Pubs
Edited by **DAVE GAMSTON**

This unique guide will lead you to nearly 120 pubs in Yorkshire and Humber which still have interiors or internal features of real historic significance. They range from simple rural 'time-warp' pubs to ornate Victorian drinking 'palaces' and include some of the more unsung pub interiors from the inter-war and later years that we take so much for granted. This revised edition of the best-selling title champions the need to celebrate, understand and protect the genuine pub heritage we have left.

£4.99   ISBN 978 1 85249 315 8

Historic Coaching Inns of the Great North Road
ROGER PROTZ

The Great North Road is part of British folklore, the Route 66 of Britain, and the magnificent coaching inns along it are part of the nation's living history. This informative traveller's guide to the coaching inns of the Great North Road takes you on a fascinating journey from London to Edinburgh and from the days of mail coaches and highwaymen right through to the modern age.

£12.99   ISBN 978 1 85249 339 4

Order these and other CAMRA books online at **www.camra.org.uk/books**, *ask your local bookstore, or contact*: CAMRA, 230 Hatfield Road, St Albans, AL1 4LW. *Telephone* 01727 867201

JOIN THE CAMPAIGN!

CAMRA, the Campaign for Real Ale, is an independent not-for-profit, volunteer-led consumer group. We promote good-quality real ale and pubs, as well as lobbying government to champion drinkers' rights and protect local pubs as centres of community life.

CAMRA has over 185,000 members from all ages and backgrounds, brought together by a common belief in the issues that CAMRA deals with and their love of good-quality British beer. From just £25 a year – that's less than a pint a month – you can join CAMRA and enjoy the following benefits:

- A monthly colour newspaper (*What's Brewing*) and award-winning quarterly magazine (*BEER*) containing news and features about beer, pubs and brewing.
- Free or reduced entry to over 200 national, regional and local beer festivals.
- Money off many of our publications including the *Good Beer Guide* and the *Good Bottled Beer Guide*.
- A 10% discount on all holidays booked with Cottages.com and Hoseasons, a 10% discount with Beer Hawk, plus much more.
- £20 worth of J D Wetherspoon real ale vouchers* (40 × 50 pence off a pint).
- Discounts in thousands of pubs across the UK through the CAMRA Real Ale Discount Scheme.
- 15 months membership for the price of 12 for new members paying by Direct Debit**

For more details about member benefits please visit **www.camra.org.uk/benefits**

If you feel passionately about your pint and about pubs, join us by visiting **www.camra.org.uk/join** or calling **01727 798 440**

For the latest campaigning news and to get involved in CAMRA's campaigns visit **www.camra.org.uk/campaigns**

*Joint members receive £20 worth of J D Wetherspoon vouchers to share.
15 months membership for the price of 12 is only available the first time a member pays by Direct Debit. **NOTE: Membership prices and benefits are subject to change.